# SLOW
# VICTORIES

———

For Tom, Lulu, Claude & Eddie: seasoned taste testers & ultimate supporters. This is for you.

x

# SLOW VICTORIES

*A Food Lover's Guide to*
## SLOW COOKER GLORY

KATRINA MEYNINK

*Hardie Grant*

BOOKS

# CONTENTS

## Soup Kitchen

## Weekend Wanderlust

## A Wee Bit Fancy

## The Sweetest Thing

# Hi there

——

I find myself writing this with some trepidation. I've spent the past year researching, testing and working on these recipes using a slow cooker, and to say responses have been divided is being subtle: something I am not normally known for. Slow cookers are either deemed irrelevant kitchen real estate, the stuff of wannabe cooks who want to remove themselves from the very act of cooking, or they are held in such high esteem that people do not want to cook without them.

I didn't know where this book would sit on that spectrum, until I realised it could actually sit anywhere. And everywhere. Whether you pull your slow cooker from the back of the cupboard and dust it off, or you want to try taking it for a different spin, or even if you've never used one in your life, this book is for you. Slow cookers are for people who love to cook.

The running of life is a symphony of efforts and, too often, cooking is sacrificed in favour of all the other hectic day to day stuff. We want to dedicate time in the kitchen to cook good food, but also feel pressure to free up that time for other things. The slow cooker is a phenomenal tool; it allows us to reclaim our time and bring more flavour to our cooking, so we need to embrace it.

There is no shame in using a slow cooker. Let's just say that again: there is no shame in using a slow cooker. In fact, if you're not using one, you are missing out. There are so many great culinary rewards to be had if only we can release this harshly judged kitchen appliance from the bonds of its 1950s housewife stereotype.

My hope for this book is that it meets your needs: the need for inspiration, the need for comfort, or for something a wee bit fancy. The spirit of this food is relaxed, not too showy, but with enough contrast to sustain your interest. The recipes range from long and low cooks to ones that only take one or two hours; you really can use your slow cooker to make just about anything. The recipes that follow focus on grains and vegetables, as well as sauces and salsas that will elevate any salad, sandwich or protein you make to something special. There are recipes for kale (ones you don't have to pretend you like). And there are a few desserts. And chocolate. Extreme dieting has no place here.

Like the slow cooker itself, these recipes are designed to nurture and build, slowly layering flavour and care into food that has the ability to inspire and bring you pleasure, connection and joy.

## Happy cooking,

*Katrina xx*

# About me

A love of cooking came to me late in life. I survived school at a time when little emphasis was placed on the arts and creative endeavours and more on generating doctors, lawyers and bankers. I went on to university, uninspired, but following the path towards getting a 'real job'. And then, instead of studying, I found myself cooking. First as a means of avoidance, then purely to satisfy this whole other part of me that needed 'feeding'.

The kneading of dough or the slow stir of a risotto was not only a beautiful distraction but a balm for my uninspired mind. And from there it grew. Instead of worrying about balancing profit and loss statements in accounting, I was preoccupied with the rise on my sourdough starter, or the reaction of my study group to the chocolate, whisky and spelt cookies I had baked for them. Without even realising it, this was my slow wake-up call; one that took layers of life to come to fruition.

I persevered with that business degree. And the journalism one, among others, that followed. I cooked, night and day, around them. Then, late one night, I discovered the James Beard Foundation, USA, and randomly applied for a scholarship. I got it. That helped pay for a Masters in Gastronomy. Then two more after that helped me get through culinary school at Le Cordon Bleu, and a Julia Child Foundation research grant made my dream of researching in Paris a reality. Slowly but surely, food became my 'real' job outside of performing my other job. Finally, I got to align the acts of writing about food with the extremely human business of eating it, and it has been a privilege every day since.

Outside of Australia, it has led to work in Dublin, New York and Paris. I have met and worked (and continue to) with incredible people in that warm, honest and genuine way that only food can facilitate.

People often tell me I am lucky that I get to do what I love. And I truly, truly am. But that also undermines the hard work, the late nights, the rejection and the prolific self-doubt that comes with travelling a less-prescribed career path. That wasn't luck. I consider that to be sheer, dogged determination; a pure and intense rejection of giving up. And I would do it all again in an instant if it meant I was given the opportunity to share one more recipe with you. Because I really like lunch, I love dinner and I've been known to be pretty partial to breakfast, too. I adore these meals just as much as I adore all the others that fall in between. I care about ingredients and great cooking, and the effort put into meals by me feeding you and you feeding me. The idea of friends and family sharing food around a table makes me feel alive. It's the sweet spot; a place of joy, one that is noisy, full of laughter, tears and fights over the salt – all of us joined together by food. Because that is ultimately what food is about: love, sharing, connecting and nurturing. It is the stuff of life, and I plan on being here for it until the end of my days.

# Some slow cooking
# COMMANDMENTS

I used many different slow cookers while developing these recipes and, like any kitchen device, they all have their quirks, advantages and pitfalls. When you know and understand what your slow cooker can and can't do, you can use it to wondrous effect.

## IT'S ALL ABOUT THE HEAT

You can buy a slow cooker for $20, but keep in mind that a slow cooker is, essentially, a transportable oven, and I believe you get what you pay for.

Spend a little more if you can on a cooker with numerous functions, most importantly, the sauté/sear function. This allows you to control the heat, and that pays dividends when you start and finish a dish in the one bowl. Nine times out of ten, the recipes in this book start with browning or sautéing in the bowl of the slow cooker. This process of caramelisation is key to building flavour, so if you keep everything in the bowl of your slow cooker, you are maximising flavour from the outset, rather than losing it in the transfer from frying pan to slow cooker.

If your slow cooker doesn't have a sauté function, don't panic. Where the recipes direct you to sauté in the bowl of the slow cooker, you can simply prepare these few elements in a frying pan on the stove and thoroughly scrape them into the bowl of your slow cooker.

After cooking (a lot) with some common-brand slow cookers and borrowing cookers new and old, I can confirm that they vary in heat. So, here are a few tips before you start:

- Older cookers run cooler than their newer counterparts. So, while a vintage slow cooker might look good on your kitchen bench, it will take longer for the food to cook, change the final outcome and consistency of the dish, and it might also sit around the temperatures that you don't want: ones where bacteria and all the funky weird stuff can lurk and grow. If you are really going to get involved with your slow cooking, I suggest a newer version.

- As a general rule of thumb, your slow cooker should have three main temperatures:

**WARM:** 65–75°C (149–167°F)
**LOW:** 80–90°C (176–194°F)
**HIGH:** 92–100°C (BOILING) (197–212°F)

- Cheaper cookers have more variability in temperature. They are often more simplistic in construction, so they take longer to heat up and, when they do, the temperature is often too high for that nice low simmer you are looking for. They also take a lot longer to cool if you need to reduce the heat quickly or hold your food on the warm setting.

• Like an oven that has temperaments and hot spots, so too does your slow cooker. The best way to overcome this is with use. The more you use your slow cooker, the more you will understand how it behaves. The recipes in this book need to be used as a guide.

• The first few times you cook a recipe in your slow cooker, take note of how long it takes to actually cook compared to the suggested cooking time in the recipe. Perhaps also note the liquid: has it reduced much? Was there too much or too little at the end of the specified time? If

your cooker runs hot, you may need to reduce the cooking time, and vice versa.

## KNOW THE LIMITS

There are some key things to embrace to get the most out of your slow cooker and maximise the culinary wins.

### Back to base

Generally speaking, the adage of throwing everything in the pot and walking away is not your friend when it comes to flavour. Long, slow cooking mellows ▶

flavours and this, combined with the lack of evaporation (and, in turn, those concentrated flavours you get from reducing something), means that your food has the potential to be bland.

Slow cooking works by building on a base flavour. The flavours in a dish need to be layered and then heightened by the use of strong spices, herbs and acid. The quantities of aromatics in the recipes may seem large, but this is deliberate.

To get maximum flavour into your base, don't rush the browning and caramelising of ingredients at the beginning. Here are a few hard-and-fast rules I like to follow:

- Always caramelise onions. It is important that you don't rush this step; onions need time to soften, lose their moisture and break down their fibres so they melt into the dish.

- Include freshly ground spices where possible. They tend to be stronger in flavour than the pre-ground versions whose oils have oxidised, which means less intensity of flavour.

- Always thoroughly cook a mirepoix (that's the carrot, celery and onion base). If you take an extra 10 minutes to cook down your aromatics, the finished dish will have a deeper flavour and a better texture.

- Always use a stock as your liquid base, rarely water.

- Sear meat until it has a nice caramelised crust.

- Heat your slow cooker before you start. You can achieve this by simply putting it on the warm function while you prepare the ingredients for the dish.

## HOW TO CONTROL LIQUIDS IN THE SLOW COOKER

The main benefit of slow cooking is the moisture that is created. It is why this method of cooking is so effective at producing mouth-watering dishes. But you need to keep a handle on it to avoid your food becoming waterlogged and to help maximise flavour and control the amount of liquid.

- Add your liquids slowly. Slow cookers love to hold onto liquid – that is both their blessing and their curse – and liquid will circulate as things steam and condensation falls back into the dish. The lids on slow cookers have almost a vacuum seal, similar to a well-sealed Dutch oven, meaning not much steam escapes. If your dish seems overly liquidy, don't panic – I have listed some simple ways to deal with too much liquid below.

- Line your lid. You can reduce the amount of liquid that makes its way back into a dish (this is particularly relevant for baking) by lining the lid. You can use a thin tea towel (dish towel) or even paper towel. This will soak up the steam and prevent it from dripping back down in the form of condensation.

- Set the lid to the side or leave it off entirely. You will note some of the recipes recommend adjusting your lid for certain amounts of time. Obviously, this isn't in the guidebook for any slow cookers because no manufacturer wants to be responsible and there is an inane fear that raw food won't get hot enough to be safe to eat. I have never found this to be true and quite often leave lids on, off and partially skewed to achieve the best end result. I encourage you to do the same and get to know how your slow cooker behaves.

- And, lastly, I'll say it again: sauté your aromatics. Do not throw raw onion, garlic and other elements into the slow cooker; they will retain a funky crunch and give off a bucketload of liquid, ruining the end result. Sauté, sauté, sauté.

When adapting other recipes for your slow cooker, it's a good idea to reduce the amount of liquid you would normally use (see also page 18).

## THINGS COULD GET UGLY

Slow cooking is akin to spending too long in the sun at the beach. You might peer inside at the end and things look, well, ugly. Rough even. But don't panic; when you cook for such long periods of time there are always separated fats, brown edges and weird lumps and bumps. For a number of recipes, I suggest removing portions and using a hand-held blender to give everything a quick whiz right there in the pot. All the bits will get reincorporated and the fats will emulsify, making the sauce or soup, for example, thick and glossy.

## FINISH WITH A BANG

Most recipes in this book finish with an array of adornments. This is the last and crucial pitstop for flavour – think herbs, nuts, acids, cooling yoghurts and creams, or mounds of cheese. These are not simply garnishes to dress up your dish and add a final flourish, but bona fide components in their own right. Always taste for salt, sour, sweet, fresh and rich before you serve.

## RECIPE NOTES

This book uses 250 ml (8½ fl oz) cups and 15 ml (½ fl oz) tablespoons. Oven temperatures are for conventional ovens, if using a fan-forced oven, reduce the oven temperature by 20°C (70°F).

Unless otherwise specified, all recipes in this book should be cooked with the slow cooker lid on.

# MY TOP 3 SLOW COOKERS

The following recommendations have not been endorsed by the manufacturers, they just come from me after using plenty of different slow cooker models in the testing for this book. And really, if you are going to invest in one, surely you want some road-tested advice from an impartial source.

## 1 KitchenAid Multi-Cooker

This gives the most even cooking. The insulation helps prevent hot spots and it has plenty of settings to maximise heat control and, in turn, the number of things you can cook in it.

## 2 Breville Fast Slow Pro (Sage Fast Slow Pro)

If I had to pick a favourite, this might be it. Extremely consistent temperatures and results every time. I've found this model to sit pretty much exactly in the middle of the cooking ranges noted on page 10.

## 3 Philips All-in-One Cooker

Lots of cooking settings, which means greater temperature control, and it has possibly the easiest yoghurt-making function. The results are unparalleled and consistent.

# A few notes on
# INGREDIENTS

Slow cooking needs strong flavour bases to build on, strengthen and amalgamate. To that end, you should have a few pantry staples and a veritable spice bazaar at your fingertips. I cannot stress it enough: having these ingredients at the ready will be your one-two punch to slow cooking glory.

## SPICES & SEASONINGS

Baharat spice mix
Bay leaves
Cardamom (whole and ground)
Celery seeds
Chermoula spice blend
Chipotle in adobo
Dried chipotle (whole and ground)
Cinnamon sticks
Coriander seeds
Cumin seeds
Fennel seeds
Mustard seeds
Paprika (sweet and smoked)
Aleppo pepper
Pink peppercorns
Sichuan peppercorns
Salt flakes
Turmeric
Urfa biber (Turkish red pepper flakes)
Vanilla bean paste

## PANTRY & PRODUCE STAPLES

Chilli
Chilli sauce
Coconut milk and cream
Cream
Eggs
Ginger
Honey
Lemons
Limes
Full-cream (whole) milk
Olive oil
Preserved lemons

Pumpkin (squash)
Rapeseed oil
Soy sauce
Superb-quality stock – vegetable
   and chicken
Sweet potato
Good-quality tinned chopped
   tomatoes
Tomato paste (concentrated purée)
Apple-cider vinegar
Chinese black vinegar

## ALLIUMS

Black garlic
Garlic
Leeks
Brown onions
Red onions
Shallots

## GRAINS & BEANS

Cannellini beans
White beans
Buckwheat
Burghul (bulgur wheat)
Chickpeas (also tinned chickpeas)
Farro
Freekeh
Brown lentils
Red lentils
Millet
Pearl barley
Quinoa (all colours)
Basmati rice
Wild rice

## AN IMPORTANT NOTE ABOUT BEANS

In this book I have used dried white beans and chickpeas, among other pulses. I haven't soaked them overnight. Instead, I let the slow cooker do the breaking down for me. This is contentious because there is some concern around the possibility of food poisoning from beans, which contain the plant lectin phytohaemagglutinin. This protein can be toxic at high levels, so the usual advice is to soak your beans in cold water overnight and boil them briefly before using. However, the beans I have used in these recipes have the lowest rate of lectin across all bean varieties, and most of the newer generation of slow cookers run at higher temperatures, eliminating the risk of food poisoning. To be safe, I recommend boiling your dried legumes for 10 minutes before proceeding with the recipe.

*A Few Notes on Ingredients*

# Slow cooker HACKS

**1** **Perfectly melt chocolate** and prevent burning. Add the chocolate to jars, place them in the slow cooker, then pour in enough water to come three-quarters of the way up the jars. Cook on low for 1 hour.

**2** **Swap out stock** for beer or even coffee for a stronger, heartier flavour in less time.

**3** **It's great for poaching.** There's no danger of boiling water in your slow cooker, so it makes an ideal environment for gentle poaching. Think of it as a pseudo sous-vide machine.

**4** **Use it as a smoker.** While you are never going to achieve the same authentic smoky flavour as you would using a proper smoker or barbecue, you can introduce a smoky flavour to your cooking by incorporating wood chips at the base of your cooker as part of the braising process.

Soak 1–2 cups wood chips (I like hickory) in water for 30 minutes, then drain. Place the chips on a sheet of baking paper, gathering up the edges to enclose the chips and make a packet that will sit in the base of the cooker. Make a few small incisions in the bag with a sharp knife or pair of scissors to allow the steam to escape. Place the bag in the base of the cooker and put your protein, or whatever you are cooking, directly on top. Pour 250 ml (8½ fl oz/ 1 cup) liquid into the base of the cooker to create a little steam, but not enough to swamp the wood chips.

**5** **Eggs for binding.** Eggs will always help to bind a sauce and are best suited to white, creamy sauces. Mix an egg with some flour to create a roux before adding liquid to create a sauce, or simply whisk in an egg yolk to help bind and thicken sauces or soups.

**6** **Use it for proving.** Fill your slow cooker halfway with water and set to the low setting. Put the lid on upside down, lay a tea towel (dish towel) on top, then set your bowl of dough in the lid. The radiant heat from the hot water below will help the dough to rise.

**7** **Brining.** Brine leaner cuts of meat before cooking to stop them drying out during the low, slow cook. For a very basic brine, add 80 g (2¾ oz) salt to 1 litre (34 fl oz/4 cups) water and stir to dissolve. You can also add aromatics. Brine the meat in the fridge overnight.

**8** **Add a steaming basket** and some water to the base of the bowl and use to steam dumplings. Or simply place a bunch of herbs and greens directly into the steamer basket and place a piece of fish on top of that. The fish steams in the moisture from the herbs below – no liquid required.

**9** **Use it as a large steamer.** Build a platform (most slow cookers come with a stand or platform insert that can be used for this) in the slow cooker's bowl, place the food on top, then fill with water until just under the top of the platform.

# How to adapt recipes for your SLOW COOKER

You can adapt so many recipes for your slow cooker. The two key things to keep in mind are liquid and time. When converting a recipe for the slow cooker, you will always need to reduce the amount of liquid specified and increase the cooking time. Below is a bit of a helpful guide.

## THINK ABOUT THE RECIPE

Not all recipes are going to work. Soups, braises, slow-cooked casseroles – these are your friends. These dishes can be more easily converted for your slow cooker sans recipe.

## CHECK THE COOKING TIME

Slow cookers gradually come to temperature and then hold that temperature for however long you tell them to. The theory is that the end result will be the same whether you cook something on high or low heat. On high, the cooker comes up to temperature quickly, whereas on low, it will heat more slowly. Which setting you use depends on the time available to cook the recipe, but I do suggest embracing the slow option, as this gives the flavours a long and luxurious amount of time to meld and intensify. As a general rule of thumb:

| Conventional oven or stove cooking time | Slow cooker cooking time on high | Slow cooker cooking time on low |
| --- | --- | --- |
| 15–30 minutes | 2 hours | 4–6 hours |
| 30–45 minutes | 2½–3 hours | 6–8 hours |
| 45 minutes–3 hours | 4–5 hours | 6–8 hours |
| 3 hours+ | 8 hours | 10–12 hours |

So, if the original cooking time was 1 hour, it should take approximately 4 hours on the high setting and no more than 6 hours on the low setting. Think pasta casseroles, quicker-style soups, chicken or seafood and veggie-loaded dishes. If the original cooking time was for more than an hour, you'll often find that it does well when cooked for 8 hours on low. This is ideal for your meat braises and slower simmered stews, such as beef bourguignon or chilli.

### REDUCE THE LIQUID

Slow cookers are little insulators, meaning a lot of liquid is created during the cooking process. Unlike a conventional oven, which allows liquid to evaporate, a slow cooker traps it. You will need to take this into account when converting a recipe and reduce the amount of liquid you use, or risk having a runny mess with reduced flavour at the end. A good rule of thumb is to decrease the liquid (wine, stock, water) in a recipe by at least 125–250 ml (4–8½ fl oz/½–1 cup).

# Condiments, Stocks & Bits & Bobs

**THERE IS A REASON** that chefs spend so damn long learning what are traditionally known as the 'mother sauces', and I could wax lyrical all day about decent sauces or condiments being the most important elements in your cooking arsenal. They serve as a flavour base that you can build on and adapt with what you have on hand, depending on the number of mouths you need to feed and the level of effort you want to apply. Condiments really are king.

# Confit tomatoes, black garlic & rosemary

MAKES APPROXIMATELY 1 LITRE (34 FL OZ/4 CUPS)

S low cookers are perfect for confit anything, as they maintain a controlled, low temperature. A confit is an excellent way to preserve flavour and shelf life and, in this recipe, it accentuates the sweetness of those last-gasp summer tomatoes. I use them in salads, over grains and proteins, spread across a pizza base or tossed through pasta. They are a must in the quest for adding easy flavour.

## Ingredients

1 head of black garlic, cloves peeled

500 g (1 lb 2 oz) mixed tomatoes

500 g (1 lb 2 oz) roma (plum) tomatoes

olive oil, to cover

1 tablespoon picked rosemary leaves

1 heaped teaspoon salt flakes

## Method

Set the slow cooker to low. Combine all the ingredients, except the salt, in the bowl of the slow cooker. Place in the warmed cooker and sprinkle over the salt. Cover with the lid and cook for 12 hours. Remove and gently spoon into sterilised jars (see below). These tomatoes will keep, covered, in the fridge for up to 1 month.

**Note** / To sterilise glass jars, simply wash them and their lids in hot, soapy water. Place the jars on a tray in a low oven and put the lids on a clean cloth or tea towel (dish towel) and leave to dry completely.

# Soffrito

MAKES APPROXIMATELY 650 G (1 LB 7 OZ/2½ CUPS)

A jar of this stuff lurking in your fridge is a call to arms come dinner time. It forms the base for so many sauces, and where a recipe might sauté aromatics at the beginning, you can simply substitute with soffrito if you are confident to do so. On its own, it is very simple – the idea being that you can add garlic or chillies or tomato later on (depending on the flavour profile of the finished dish). The long, slow cook means the oil takes on the deep flavours of the vegetables as they caramelise, adding an extra depth of flavour to your cooking.

## Ingredients

250 ml (8½ fl oz/1 cup) excellent-quality
  olive oil
2 onions, finely chopped
1 large celery stalk, finely chopped
1 large carrot, finely chopped
1 teaspoon salt flakes

## Method

Set the slow cooker to the sauté function. Add the oil and, once hot, add the onion, celery and carrot. Close the lid and cook for 8 hours on low. Taste and season with the salt. Transfer to an airtight container, making sure that the vegetables are completely submerged in the oil. This will keep in the fridge for up to 1 month.

# The ultimate 8-hour pepper sauce

MAKES 500 ML (17 FL OZ/2 CUPS)

A pepper sauce that cooks for 8 hours? I know it seems crazy, but this languid slow cook allows all the flavours to meld and mellow and do their thing. I saw chef Matt Sinclair making pepper sauce using oyster sauce and knew I had to come up with a version for the slow cooker. The oyster sauce adds the most wonderful rounded umami flavour to this old-school favourite. I also use a mixture of peppers – probably overkill, so if you don't have them, just use black pepper. It will still be amazing.

Serve this sauce with a bit of grilled steak or toss it through some fresh pasta – the opportunities are endless. I've kept the quantities relatively small as this one doesn't freeze well, so make it for a celebration meal, or mid-week just because.

## Ingredients

1½ tablespoons olive oil

30 g (1 oz) butter

1 onion, finely chopped

2 garlic cloves, crushed

60 ml (2 fl oz/¼ cup) oyster sauce

1 tablespoon pink peppercorns

1 tablespoon black peppercorns

170 ml (5½ fl oz/⅔ cup) chicken or vegetable stock

500 ml (17 fl oz/2 cups) pouring (single/light) cream

## Method

Set the slow cooker to the sauté function. Add the oil and butter and, once the butter has melted and is foaming, add the onion and garlic and cook for 3 minutes, or until the onion is translucent. Add the oyster sauce and cook until reduced a little and it appears to be almost coating the onion. Roughly grind the peppercorns with a mortar and pestle (not too much; you still want chunky pieces) and add to the bowl. Add the stock and cream, and stir to combine. Set the heat to low and cook for 8 hours. You can also turn this off at the 6-hour mark if time isn't on your side.

# Smoky gochujang barbecue sauce

MAKES 1 LITRE (34 FL OZ/4 CUPS)

I've erred on the side of caution here: the intensity of gochujang paste can vary, so add the amount suggested below and reassess when you taste at the end. You can always stir through more depending on your preference.

## Ingredients

1 tablespoon olive oil

1 onion, finely chopped

2 garlic cloves, chopped

1 teaspoon each of ground fennel, coriander, celery seeds, mustard seeds

200 ml (7 fl oz) apple purée

125 ml (4 fl oz/½ cup) apple-cider vinegar

55 g (2 oz/¼ cup, firmly packed) brown sugar, plus extra if needed

50 g (1¾ oz) tinned chipotle in adobo, chopped

2 × 400 g (14 oz) tins crushed tomatoes

125 ml (4 fl oz/½ cup) maple syrup

3 teaspoons gochujang (Korean chilli paste), or to taste

## Method

Set the slow cooker to the sauté function. Add the oil and, once hot, add the onion and cook until clear and translucent, about 5 minutes. Add the garlic and the spices and cook, stirring often to prevent them catching, until fragrant. Add the remaining ingredients, cover with the lid and cook for 4 hours on high. Taste and adjust the seasoning with sugar, salt and pepper. Also taste for heat and stir through a little more gochujang if necessary. Blitz using a hand-held blender, or allow to cool then purée using a food processor. Seal in airtight, sterilised screw-top jars (see Note on page 23) and store in the fridge for up to 4 weeks, or freeze for up to 3 months.

# Dulce de leche (heavy on the vanilla)

MAKES 520 G (1 LB 2 OZ)

If, like me, you are one of the 0.6 per cent of people who have managed to blow up a tin of condensed milk trying to reduce it in a pot of boiling water, then this recipe is your new best friend. This slow (and safe) method thickens and darkens the milk to look much like its traditional South American counterpart. Use it for the Sticky date cake with dulce de leche (page 206), pour it indecently over ice cream, or, my personal favourite, eat it straight from the fridge with a spoon.

## Ingredients

2 × 395 g (14 oz) tins condensed milk

250 ml (8½ fl oz/1 cup) full-cream (whole) milk

2½ tablespoons vanilla bean paste

1 teaspoon salt flakes

## Method

Add all the ingredients to the bowl of the slow cooker and give everything a good stir. Set to low and cook for 8 hours. If you like your caramel deep and dark, you can extend this to 10, just make sure you stir it fairly regularly. As it cooks, and particularly towards the end, you will find the caramel becomes particularly lumpy and bumpy. Don't panic. At the end of cooking, allow it to cool slightly before pouring into a blender and giving it a quick blitz to smooth out (you can also use a hand-held blender).

Dulce de leche will keep in a tightly sealed sterilised glass jar (see Note on page 23) in the fridge for up to 1 month.

# Yoghurt

MAKES 2–2½ KG (4 LB 6 OZ–5½ LB/8–10 CUPS)

With three small people to feed who are obsessed with yoghurt, I was spending a mortgage repayment on tubs of the stuff each week. I have tried all the yoghurt makers out there and have, time and again, been left with a weird, watery mess, or something mouth-cloyingly sweet that was no better than the shop-bought stuff. Enter the slow cooker. My mind was blown. I'll admit, it's a bit fiddly to start with, but once you've made it a few times, you won't even blink.

**A few tips:**
- Add 100 g (3½ oz/1 cup) powdered milk to the quantities below for a thick, luscious Greek-style yoghurt.
- If using alternative milks, such as nut or oat milk, you will need to add sugar for the bacteria to activate, and you will need some yoghurt culture. You can find this online or at some gourmet grocers.
- You can halve this recipe for a smaller batch.

## Ingredients

2 litres (68 fl oz/8 cups) full-cream (whole) milk, at room temperature

500 g (1 lb 2 oz/2 cups) yoghurt with live cultures, at room temperature

2 tablespoons caster (superfine) sugar (optional; omit if making yoghurt to serve with savoury dishes)

2 teaspoons vanilla bean paste (optional; omit if making yoghurt to serve with savoury dishes)

## Method

Add the milk to your slow cooker and set to low. The aim is to heat it to just over 80°C (176°F). If you wanted to speed things up, you could heat the milk on the stovetop and then pour it into the slow cooker. Once at the correct temperature, turn off the cooker and let it sit for about 1 hour to cool. Check regularly – you want the temperature to come down to about 40°C (104°F) or just over. The main reason for heating the milk before fermenting it is that it improves the yoghurt texture.

  Add the remaining ingredients and whisk to combine. Keep the bowl in the cooker as this is the perfect warm hug that it needs, then cover with the lid. You want to ensure it stays in a warm place for at least 8 hours, around 40°C (104°F) or just over. Alternatively, you can wrap your slow cooker in a towel and pop it somewhere draft free for 6–8 hours. If the yoghurt still seems a little runny, you can incubate it for another 4–6 hours. Strain it using a piece of muslin (cheesecloth) to eliminate the extra whey. At this point, you can return the yoghurt to the slow cooker and let it sit for an additional 2 hours to achieve an even thicker consistency.

**Note** / The Philips All-in-One Cooker has a yoghurt function. If you happen to have this slow cooker, the results are consistent and foolproof. You literally put everything in, close the lid and have yoghurt 10 hours later. It is a game changer and I would buy the unit for this function alone.

# Strawberry, hibiscus & pomegranate jam

MAKES APPROXIMATELY 945 G (2 LB 1 OZ/3 CUPS)

I have a complicated relationship with jam. I go from seeking out its mouth-coating sweetness for a butter-addled crumpet to wishing it away to the darkest recesses of my fridge. I feel like this jam is the middle ground; the Switzerland of jams – most definitely sweet but with these delightful punches of background tang thanks to the pomegranate molasses.

## Ingredients

200 g (7 oz) jar hibiscus flowers in syrup

750 g (1 lb 11 oz) strawberries, hulled

3 tablespoons pomegranate molasses

115 g (4 oz/½ cup) caster (superfine) sugar

1 heaped teaspoon vanilla bean paste

## Method

Place all the ingredients in the bowl of your slow cooker and stir to combine. Cover and cook for 2½ hours on low. Open the lid and give it a good stir to allow some of the steam to escape. Continue cooking for another 45–60 minutes until the mixture resembles a nice relish; a bit runnier than a jam. This is going to vary between slow cookers, so check on it a few times the first time you make it and note how long it takes in your cooker.

Transfer to sterilised glass jars (see Note on page 23) and store in the fridge for up to 3 months.

You will need a large-volume slow cooker for this recipe

# Lockdown sauce

**MAKES 1.5 LITRES (51 FL OZ/6 CUPS)**

I created this recipe for the lovely readers of a food newspaper, and I knew I had to adapt it for the slow cooker. It came about in the thick of the Coronavirus outbreak and it seemed to really resonate with people. There is something so infinitely useful about a standard base sauce; it can take your cooking anywhere, and this is one I strongly suggest you include in your repertoire. It also freezes well, so make a big batch and divide it up to store for later use.

## Ingredients

2 tablespoons olive oil

2 red onions, finely chopped

140 g (5 oz/1 cup) finely chopped celery

2 carrots, finely chopped

4 garlic cloves, crushed

1 tablespoon thyme leaves

4 × 400 g (14 oz) tins crushed tomatoes

500 ml (17 fl oz/2 cups) white wine

500 ml (17 fl oz/2 cups) chicken stock

2 tablespoons brown sugar

1 tablespoon balsamic vinegar

1 tablespoon white miso (optional)

## Method

Set your slow cooker to the sauté function. Add the oil and, when nice and hot, add the onion, celery, carrot and garlic. As soon as you hear a sizzle, begin stirring constantly for 10 minutes, or until the onion is translucent. Add the thyme and cook for another minute or so, then add the tomatoes, wine and stock. Give it a good stir, then add the brown sugar and vinegar. Leave the lid slightly ajar and cook on low for 8 hours. Taste and adjust the seasoning accordingly.

Stir through the miso, if using, during the last 30 minutes of cooking. You want the mixture to intensify in colour and consistency. Depending on how broken down your vegetables are, use a hand-held blender to give it a quick whiz to take care of any larger chunks at the end. This will also help to thicken your sauce.

This sauce will keep in sterilised glass jars (see Note on page 23) in the fridge for up to 1 month. Use it as a base for pasta sauces, drizzled over roast chook, or even on a pizza base.

# Chunky apple, rosemary & black pepper mostarda

MAKES 625 G (1 LB 6 OZ/2½ CUPS)

This is a bit of a multi-purpose relish. It works well served simply with cheese, or slathered over oven-roasted parsnips or a slab of crisp, piping-hot pork belly.

## Ingredients

2 tablespoons olive oil

1 kg (2 lb 3 oz) sweet apples, peeled, cored and cut into chunks

1 teaspoon black peppercorns, roughly crushed

1½ teaspoons chopped rosemary

2 tablespoons brown sugar

185 g (6½ oz/¾ cup) dijon mustard

1 teaspoon apple-cider vinegar

## Method

Set the slow cooker to the sauté function. Add the oil and, once hot, add the apple with a pinch of salt, the pepper and half the rosemary. Cook until the apple is browning and starting to soften, then add the remaining ingredients, including the remaining rosemary. Close the lid and cook on low for 2 hours. Stir vigorously with a wooden spoon; you want a chunky, relish-style consistency. Adjust the seasoning to taste.

This will keep in an airtight container in the fridge for up to 2 weeks (see also Note on page 23 on sterilising jars).

# Immunity boosting, 24-hour slow-cooked chicken broth

MAKES 2 LITRES (68 FL OZ/8 CUPS)

You will need a large-volume slow cooker for this recipe

You will have a pretty spectacular broth after just 12 hours if you need it, but given the hands-off nature of cooking this way, it is easy to turn it on for another 12 hours, and it will give you something truly wondrous.

## Ingredients

bones from 2 roasted chickens

2 leeks, roughly chopped (all the bits)

3 shallots, roughly chopped

1 lemongrass stem, roughly chopped, pieces bruised

10 cm (4 in) piece ginger, chopped

5 cm (2 in) piece turmeric, thoroughly cleaned

1 tablespoon coriander seeds, roughly ground

½ tablespoon black peppercorns, roughly ground

2 star anise, bruised

1 bay leaf

1 tablespoon apple-cider vinegar

## Method

Place the chicken bones in the bowl of your slow cooker. You may need to play a bit of Tetris to ensure you fit them as snugly as possible. Scatter over the vegetables, then add the remaining ingredients and enough water to cover the chicken and vegetables, about 2 litres (68 fl oz/8 cups). Set to low and cook for 12 hours. Check the water at this point and, if you are feeling energetic, skim any foam from the surface. Add more water if required, just enough to cover, and continue cooking for another 12 hours.

Set a strainer lined with a piece of muslin (cheesecloth) over a large bowl. Remove the big bones and chunkier vegetables with tongs, then gently strain the stock. Divide between sterilised glass jars (see Note on page 23) and seal. This lasts in the fridge for about 1 week, and roughly 3 months in the freezer.

# Enchilada sauce

**MAKES 1 LITRE (34 FL OZ/4 CUPS)**

This enchilada sauce is really easy and worth a bit of planning to ensure you have it on hand. It elevates a simple, homely meal by adding depth of flavour without all those weird ingredients you find in many of the packaged Mexican foods. Better yet, you should find most of the ingredients for this already lurking in your cupboard.

I picked up the trick of making a cheat's roux from oil and flour from a chef in cooking school, and I often find myself using it when time is against me. It makes a gloriously thick sauce, and there's no need to stand over it stirring constantly.

## Ingredients

2 tablespoons rice bran oil

2 tablespoons plain (all-purpose) flour

500 ml (17 fl oz/2 cups) chicken stock

1 × 400 g (14 oz) tin crushed tomatoes

1 tablespoon tomato paste (concentrated purée)

½ tablespoon brown sugar

½ tablespoon each of dried oregano, ground cumin, sweet smoked paprika, chipotle powder, ground coriander

2 garlic cloves, crushed

1 teaspoon salt flakes

## Method

Set the slow cooker to the sauté function. Add the oil and flour and whisk until combined, almost as if you are making a roux. It will thicken as the slow cooker comes up to heat. Add the remaining ingredients, set the heat to low and cook for 8 hours, with the lid slightly askew for the last 2 hours of cooking.

Divide between sterilised glass jars (see Note on page 23) and seal. This lasts in the fridge for about 1 week, and roughly 3 months in the freezer.

# Vegetable compost stock

**MAKES 2 LITRES (68 FL OZ/8 CUPS)**

You will need a large-volume slow cooker for this recipe

This is basically the remnants of your crisper, or the vegetable trimmings from your cooking, collected and used instead of simply tossing them in the compost or bin. You can use whatever you have on hand, just stay away from the likes of cabbage, broccoli or cauliflower; these cruciferous veggies tend to leave a weird, almost bitter flavour. It's subtle, but best to avoid if you can. Keep your vegetable trimmings in a sealed container in the fridge until you have collected 700 g (1 lb 9 oz). You will be surprised at how quickly it comes together.

## Ingredients

3 tablespoons olive oil

6 garlic cloves, peeled

2 onions, chopped

3 carrots, roughly chopped

3 celery stalks, chopped

700 g (1 lb 9 oz) vegetable scraps
   (see introduction)

1 tablespoon liquid kombu (you can
   find this at Asian grocers)

½ tablespoon black peppercorns

8 cm (3¼ in) piece ginger, sliced

3 bay leaves

## Method

Set the slow cooker to the sauté function. Add the oil and, once hot, add the garlic, onion, carrot and celery. Cook until fragrant and soft. Add all the remaining ingredients, plus about 2 litres (68 fl oz/8 cups) water, or enough to generously cover. Give everything a gentle stir, then close the lid and cook on low for 8 hours. Strain the stock into sterilised glass jars (see Note on page 23) and refrigerate for up to 2 weeks. Alternatively, you can freeze the stock in ice-cube trays or measured cups for future use. It will last in the freezer for up to 6 months.

# Better than Botox: Beef bone broth

**MAKES 1.5–2 LITRES (51–68 FL OZ/6–8 CUPS)**

You will need
a large-volume
slow cooker for
this recipe

So. Much. Collagen. No idea if edible collagen is really a thing after it's been given a rinse by our stomach acids, but I like to dream big. Regardless of its skin- and hair-boosting effects, it adds absolutely wonderful flavour and silky texture to whatever you cook with it. There really is no comparison to making your own.

## Ingredients

2 kg (4 lb 6 oz) beef bones

6 lemon thyme sprigs

2 tablespoons apple-cider vinegar

2 carrots, roughly chopped

1 onion, halved

2 celery stalks, chopped

1 teaspoon coriander seeds,
   roughly crushed

1 teaspoon black peppercorns

6 garlic cloves

2 bay leaves

## Method

Roast the beef bones on a roasting tray in a 180°C (350°F) oven until dark and golden. Scrape the bones and any cooking juices and gnarly bits into the bowl of your slow cooker. Top with the remaining ingredients, pushing them down so they're nice and snug in your cooker. Add just enough water to cover the ingredients. Set the heat to low and cook for 12 hours. It is good to go at this point, but if you would like deeper flavours, cook for an additional 12 hours – just check the liquid after 12 hours and add a touch more water if required.

Remove the bones and chunkier bits of vegetables from the broth using tongs. Place a strainer lined with a piece of muslin (cheesecloth) over a large bowl and gently strain the broth, then store in sterilised glass jars (see Note on page 23). This will keep for approximately 1 week in the fridge and up to 4 months in the freezer.

# Grain Fed

PEOPLE'S VIEW ON SLOW cookers seems to fall into two camps: there are those who dismiss them altogether as madness or cheating in the kitchen, and there are those so in love with them that it is almost a religion. If ever anything was going to convert you to the latter group, let it be the cooking of grains. There is no stirring, no rapid evaporation of liquid and subsequent ruining of saucepans. Instead, the controlled heat and evaporation make for perfect, fluffy grains. As someone who adores grains in all their forms, I have found this to be life changing.

I highly recommend closely observing the cooking of your grains the first few times you try this and keep note of how long they take to cook and how quickly the liquid is absorbed, as this can vary dramatically between slow cookers. As a general guide, I found 1 hour to be pretty much on the money with most cookers – and the recipes reflect this – but I urge you to check and then adapt accordingly for your cooker.

# Freekeh with kale, chilli, yeast & pepita salad

**SERVES 2 AS A MAIN OR 4 AS A SIDE**

I'm just going to say this up front: the nutritional yeast in this salad is a revelation. It truly adds the most phenomenal umami flavour, as well as being a superb seasoning mechanism. This salad has excellent holding power, so it's always a good one for work lunches or those irksome bring-a-plate scenarios.

## Ingredients

200 g (7 oz/1 cup) whole freekeh, rinsed

500 ml (17 fl oz/2 cups) vegetable stock

### Salad

50 g (1¾ oz/1 cup) nutritional yeast flakes

150 g (5½ oz/1 cup) salted pepitas
  (pumpkin seeds), roughly chopped
  (see Note)

125–185 ml (4–6 fl oz/½–¾ cup) olive oil

150 g (5½ oz/2 cups) cavolo nero,
  finely sliced

1 green chilli, finely sliced

baby cavolo nero leaves, to garnish
  (optional)

## Method

Heat your slow cooker on the low setting for at least 20 minutes. Add the freekeh and vegetable stock, give it a good stir, then cover and cook on low for 1 hour. Check it at the 45-minute mark and if there still seems to be quite a lot of stock, leave the lid off for the last 15–20 minutes. Once cooked, fluff with a fork. (It should be cooked through, but al dente.) Turn out into a bowl and season generously with salt and pepper, then allow to cool.

For the salad, add the nutritional yeast, pepitas and 125 ml (4 fl oz) of the oil to another bowl and stir to combine. If the mixture looks too dry, add more oil until it reaches a lose pesto-like consistency. Add the cavolo nero and chilli and toss with your hands. Add the freekeh, season again with salt and pepper, and garnish with baby cavolo nero leaves, if using, then serve. If you need to revive this for another day, simply slice some more cavolo nero and toss it through.

**Note** / Use unsalted pepitas if you prefer. You can even add these to a mortar and pestle and give them a rough grind; it works wonders.

# Turmeric herb chickpeas & rice

SERVES 4

This is the kind of superbly simple, healthy dinner that you can throw together in an instant. This recipe uses dried chickpeas, but if time is against you, you could wash and strain a tin of chickpeas, reduce the cooking time to about 1 hour and reduce the amount of stock by just over half.

If you are concerned about the lectin in dried beans, see page 15 for preparation instructions.

## Ingredients

2 tablespoons olive oil

1 onion, finely chopped

3 garlic cloves, crushed

5 cm (2 in) piece ginger, finely sliced

3 teaspoons freshly grated turmeric, or
1½ generous teaspoons ground turmeric

250 g (9 oz/generous cup) dried chickpeas

¼ preserved lemon, finely chopped

750 ml (25½ fl oz/3 cups) vegetable or
chicken stock, plus extra if needed

3 tablespoons sultanas (golden raisins)

370 g (13 oz/2 cups) cooked white rice

### Herb stir-through

100 g (3½ oz/2 cups) baby spinach

½ bunch coriander (cilantro),
leaves roughly chopped

handful of dill fronds

½ bunch flat-leaf (Italian) parsley,
roughly chopped

2 tablespoons marjoram or lemon thyme
leaves

### To serve

Greek or coconut yoghurt (page 30)

coriander (cilantro) leaves

## Method

Set the slow cooker to the sauté function. Add the oil and, once shimmering, add the onion and cook until translucent and fragrant, about 5 minutes. Add the garlic, ginger and turmeric and cook for another minute. Add the chickpeas and preserved lemon and cook until coated in the mixture. Add the stock, cover with the lid and cook for 8–10 hours on low. Add the sultanas for the last 20 minutes of cooking, along with a splash more stock if the chickpeas have absorbed all the liquid.

Stir in the cooked rice, adding more stock again if necessary, to create a slightly loose, stew-like consistency. Cook for an additional minute, then remove from the heat and stir through the spinach and herbs. Let it rest for 1 minute to allow the spinach to soften, then add a dollop of Greek yoghurt. Season to taste and serve with a few extra coriander leaves.

# Rose harissa millet with chickpeas, almonds & dill

SERVES 2 AS A MAIN OR 4 AS A SIDE

Throw in the ingredients. Turn on the cooker. Leave it for 1 hour. Throw herbs and nuts at it. Meal done. This is a wonderful side to most proteins, particularly lamb, chicken and white fish, and is equally marvellous as lunch the next day.

## Ingredients

190 g (6½ oz/1 cup) millet

500 ml (17 fl oz/2 cups) vegetable or chicken stock

1 garlic clove, crushed

1 × 425 g (15 oz) tin chickpeas, drained and thoroughly rinsed

1 tablespoon rose harissa

155 g (5½ oz/1 cup) smoked almonds, roughly chopped

½ bunch of dill, fronds pulled

½ bunch flat-leaf (Italian) parsley, finely chopped

75 g (2¾ oz/½ cup) currants

### To serve

Greek yoghurt (page 30)

rose harissa, for drizzling

3 tablespoons chopped spring onions (scallions)

## Method

Add the millet, stock, garlic and chickpeas and half the harissa to the bowl of your slow cooker. Give it a quick stir to combine. Close the lid and cook on low for 1 hour. The first time you make this, give it a quick stir at the 45-minute mark and check the liquid. If it has been absorbed and the grains are light and fluffy, turn out the millet and chickpeas into a bowl. If the liquid hasn't quite been absorbed, cook for another 15 minutes with the lid ajar.

Once cooked, taste and adjust the amount of rose harissa accordingly. Add the remaining ingredients and season well with salt and pepper. Dollop with yoghurt, an extra drizzle of harissa and scatter over the spring onions to serve.

# Wild rice with mushrooms, rosemary & cranberries

SERVES 6

This is the kind of wholesome and nourishing dish that invites over-eating. It just begs you to go back for seconds. And thirds.

Don't be alarmed if your dish looks a little purple; the black grains in the wild rice can sometimes leach a bit of their colour. You've done nothing wrong, it's just the variability that comes with the grain and doesn't impact the taste.

## Ingredients

1 tablespoon olive oil

1 onion, finely chopped

generous knob of butter

1 tablespoon finely chopped rosemary

180 g (6½ oz/2 cups) mixed mushrooms, finely sliced

140 g (5 oz/¾ cup) wild rice

150 g (5½ oz/¾ cup) brown basmati rice

435 ml (15 fl oz/1¾ cups) vegetable or chicken stock

85 g (3 oz/¾ cup) dried cranberries, chopped

## To serve

4–6 cavolo nero leaves, roughly torn

45 g (1½ oz/½ cup) lightly toasted flaked almonds

## Method

Set the slow cooker to the sauté function. Add the oil and, once hot, add the onion and cook for 3–5 minutes, or until translucent. Add the butter and, once the mixture appears to be foaming, add the rosemary and mushrooms. Cook for another 2 minutes before adding the rices. Cook, stirring to coat, then add the stock and cranberries. Close the lid and cook on low for 1 hour. Check the rice at the 45-minute mark; you want the stock to have been absorbed and the rice to have an ever-so-slight resistance to the bite. If you still have liquid, leave the lid off and continue to check the rice at 10-minute intervals until cooked to your liking and the liquid has been fully absorbed.

When you're ready to serve, stir the cavolo nero leaves through the warm rice to soften them. Season generously with salt and pepper, then scatter over the flaked almonds and serve.

# Mixed grains with toasted chickpeas, fig & Baharat dressing

SERVES 4 AS A MAIN OR 6 AS A SIDE

This works as a standalone meal or a wonderful side to lamb. It also has phenomenal holding power, so last night's leftovers can stretch to a few superb work lunches during the week.

## Ingredients

100 g (3½ oz/½ cup) tri-colour quinoa

110 g (4 oz/½ cup) pearl barley

100 g (3½ oz/½ cup) freekeh

625 ml (21 fl oz/2½ cups) vegetable or chicken stock

1 × 425 g (15 oz) tin chickpeas, drained and thoroughly rinsed

2 tablespoons olive oil

1 tablespoon Baharat spice mix

1 teaspoon ground coriander

3 tablespoons chopped flat-leaf (Italian) parsley

1 tablespoon dill fronds

70 g (2½ oz) smoked almonds

3 tablespoons pepitas (pumpkin seeds)

### Fig & Baharat dressing

80 g (2¾ oz/½ cup) dried figs, finely chopped

60 ml (2 fl oz/¼ cup) olive oil

juice of ½ large lemon

2 teaspoons Baharat spice mix

## Method

Place all the grains and the stock in the bowl of your slow cooker. Close the lid and cook on low for 1 hour. If there is still some liquid remaining, remove the lid and continue to cook for another 10–15 minutes, or until the grains are cooked through and all the liquid has evaporated. Set aside to cool.

Preheat the oven to 170°C (340°F).

Spread the chickpeas on a large baking tray lined with baking paper. Combine the olive oil, Baharat and coriander in a small bowl, then drizzle over the chickpeas. Roast in the oven until crisp, about 30–40 minutes.

To make the dressing, combine all the ingredients in a bowl.

Add the herbs, cooled grains and toasted chickpeas to a bowl. Toss gently to combine, then add the smoked almonds and pepitas. Toss again, then check for seasoning before drizzling over the dressing to serve.

# Loaded Mexican grain salad

SERVES 6

The perfect dunch (dinner lunch) when the day has escaped you or you just don't quite know what you fancy. This is hefty, full of flavour and can be easily adapted to include grilled chicken or prawns if you need to feed more mouths.

## Ingredients

185 g (6½ oz/1 cup) green lentils, rinsed

220 g (8 oz/1 cup) pearl barley, rinsed

875 ml–1 litre (29½–34 fl oz/3½–4 cups) vegetable stock

1 tablespoon chipotle in adobo, chopped

### Salad

250 g (9 oz) sweet solanato tomatoes, halved lengthways

120 g (4½ oz/½ cup) Persian feta

½ bunch coriander (cilantro), roughly chopped

3 tablespoons oregano, chopped

½ bunch mint leaves, roughly chopped

1 tablespoon marjoram leaves, chopped

1 tablespoon thyme leaves

1 avocado, sliced

1 corn cob, cooked, kernels sliced off

### Chipotle lime dressing

1½ teaspoons chipotle powder

zest and juice of 2 limes

125 ml (4 fl oz/½ cup) olive oil

1½ teaspoons ground cumin

1½ teaspoons brown sugar

1 garlic clove, chopped

### To serve

corn chips (optional)

## Method

Place the lentils and barley in the bowl of your slow cooker and add enough stock to cover. (To check you have enough liquid, I like to use the thumb test: you should be able to dip in your thumb to the base of your nail.) Stir through the chipotle in adobo and close the lid. Cook on low heat for 60–80 minutes. I suggest checking on it quickly around the 45-minute mark. Add a splash more stock if you think too much has been absorbed. This is never an exact science; slow cookers can vary with heat, so it is best to check at this point and add a little more if needed.

While still warm, season generously with salt and pepper, then set aside to cool.

Combine the salad ingredients and gently toss through the cooled grains.

Mix the dressing ingredients in a small bowl, then pour over the salad. Toss again to combine and season to taste.

# Quinoa lemongrass larb gai

SERVES 6

T his is the ultimate hot summer night dinner. It's light, fresh and full of punchy flavours. I would pick this vegetarian version over the traditional meat-based dish every single time.

## Ingredients

1 teaspoon rice bran oil

2 shallots, finely sliced

1 tablespoon finely grated lemongrass

5 cm (2 in) piece ginger, finely sliced

200 g (7 oz/1 cup) white quinoa

250 ml (8½ fl oz/1 cup) master stock

250 ml (8½ fl oz/1 cup) vegetable stock

## Dressing

3 tablespoons lime juice

1 tablespoon rice vinegar

1 tablespoon mirin

1 tablespoon brown sugar

1 red chilli, deseeded and finely chopped
    (use to taste)

## Dipping sauce (optional)

80 ml (2½ fl oz/⅓ cup) fresh orange juice

3 tablespoons soy sauce

3 tablespoons brown sugar

2 tablespoons lime juice

1 teaspoon sesame oil

## Herb stir-through

½ small bunch coriander (cilantro), chopped

small handful Thai basil leaves, chopped

½ small bunch mint leaves, roughly chopped

small handful Vietnamese mint leaves, chopped

2 kaffir lime leaves, very finely sliced

125 g (4½ oz/1 cup) snake (yard-long) beans,
    cut into bite-sized pieces

## To serve

iceberg lettuce or butter lettuce

fried onion

bean sprouts

sliced red chilli

## Method

Turn the slow cooker to the sauté function and immediately dump in the oil, shallot, lemongrass and ginger. Cook until just fragrant, turning regularly to prevent the lemongrass from catching and burning. Keep watching: you want just enough heat to release the oils and flavour. Add the remaining ingredients. Give it a good stir to combine, then close the lid. Cook on low for 60–70 minutes, then stir again. Turn off and leave to sit for another 10 minutes.

While the quinoa is cooking, make the dressing. Combine all the ingredients in a bowl and whisk until mixed. Set aside.

Make the dipping sauce, if using, by combining all the ingredients in a small serving bowl and stirring gently until mixed. Set aside.

To serve, stir the dressing through the quinoa, followed by the herbs, lime leaves and beans. Serve with the lettuce cups, onion, bean sprouts, chilli and dipping sauce.

# Za'atar buckwheat & farro salad with pomegranate dressing

SERVES 4

Another one with epic staying power, this is your make-ahead, bring-a-plate, got-no-idea-what-to-have-with-a-bit-of-protein kind of salad.

## Ingredients

100 g (3½ oz/½ cup) farro

110 g (4 oz/½ cup) buckwheat groats

250 ml (8½ fl oz/1 cup) vegetable or chicken stock

2 tablespoons olive oil

1 tablespoon za'atar spice blend

65 g (2¼ oz/½ cup) dried cranberries

90 g (3 oz/2 cups) finely sliced cavolo nero

180 g (6½ oz/¾ cup) Persian feta

## Dressing

3 tablespoons pomegranate molasses

2 tablespoons olive oil

## Method

Set your slow cooker to low. Add the grains and stock and stir to combine, then close the lid and cook for 1 hour. Check at the 45-minute mark: if the grains aren't quite cooked and there is still a lot of liquid, continue cooking, checking at 15-minute intervals, until the grains are fully cooked. (They should still hold their shape and have some resistance to the bite.) Open the lid slightly and let the grains sit for at least 15 minutes, then fluff with a fork.

Mix the oil and za'atar in a small bowl, then pour over the warm grains, tossing with a wooden spoon to coat. Turn out the grains into a large serving bowl and top with the cranberries, cavolo nero and feta. Using salad servers, toss gently to combine. Season generously with salt and pepper.

Combine the dressing ingredients in a small bowl and pour over the salad just before serving.

# Heirloom pumpkin & saffron stew with barley, green harissa & haloumi

SERVES 4

Feel free to use a quality shop-bought green harissa, but I have included a recipe for those who feel inclined to make it themselves. This is a very simple braise, and one that warrants the extras – I love to serve it with a mound of black barley, the harissa and a big door-stop wedge of squeaky grilled haloumi.

## Ingredients

½ teaspoon rosewater

pinch of saffron threads

60 ml (2 fl oz/¼ cup) rapeseed oil

3 shallots, chopped

1 teaspoon each of cumin and coriander
   seeds, toasted and roughly ground

1 teaspoon ground cardamom

1 × 800 g–1 kg (1 lb 12 oz–2lb 3 oz)
   butternut pumpkin (squash), peeled
   and cut into chunks

375 ml (12½ fl oz/1½ cups) vegetable
   stock, or enough to cover

¼ preserved lemon, finely chopped

## Green harissa

2 tablespoons cumin seeds, toasted
   and roughly ground

1 tablespoon coriander seeds, toasted
   and roughly ground

½ tablespoon black peppercorns,
   roughly ground

1 teaspoon ground cinnamon

7 garlic cloves, chopped

bunch of coriander (cilantro), thoroughly
   washed and chopped

handful mint leaves

80 ml (2½ fl oz/⅓ cup) olive oil, plus extra
   if needed

1 teaspoon salt flakes

## To serve

440 g (15½ oz/2 cups) cooked black barley

8 slices grilled haloumi

coriander (cilantro) leaves

## Method

To make the harissa, add all the ingredients to a food processor and blitz to combine. If it seems too thick, add a little more olive oil, 1 teaspoon at a time. Pour into a sterilised glass jar (see Note on page 23) and cover with a film of oil before sealing. Pop in the fridge until ready to use. It will keep for up to 2 weeks.

In a small bowl, combine the rosewater and saffron threads, then set aside while you prepare the remaining ingredients.

Set your slow cooker to the sauté function. Add the oil and, once hot, add the shallot and cook for about 5 minutes, or until soft and caramelised. Stir in the spices, a good pinch of salt and a good grinding of pepper. Continue to cook for another 1–2 minutes. Add the saffron and rosewater, followed by the pumpkin pieces. Pour over the stock and turn the heat to low. Cover and cook for 1–2 hours.

Serve scooped over black barley and topped with the green harissa, grilled haloumi and coriander.

# Spiced lamb burghul

SERVES 4

This is a more grain-centric and simplified version of dirty rice. I love freshening it with coriander, and you could also add mint and cucumber once cooked to bulk it out further and add more freshness and bite.

## Ingredients

2 tablespoons olive oil

500 g (1 lb 2 oz) minced (ground) lamb

2 garlic cloves, crushed

3 teaspoons cumin seeds, toasted and
   roughly ground

2 teaspoons sweet smoked paprika

1 teaspoon fennel seeds,
   roughly ground

½ teaspoon chilli flakes

1½ teaspoons ground cinnamon

pinch of allspice

175 g (6 oz/1 cup) burghul (bulgur wheat)

45 g (1½ oz/¼ cup) brown lentils

500 ml (17 fl oz/2 cups) chicken stock

## To serve

coriander (cilantro) leaves

## Method

Set your slow cooker to the sauté function and allow to warm up. Add the oil and, once hot, add the lamb in batches and cook, stirring occasionally, until golden, about 2–4 minutes. Return all the lamb to the bowl, then add the garlic and spices and cook until fragrant, about 20 seconds. Next, add the burghul and lentils, followed by the stock. Stir to combine, then close the lid and cook on low for 1 hour.

Remove the bowl from the heat and give everything a good stir. The stock should have been absorbed and the burghul should be quite fluffy.

As with most recipes in this book, I suggest the first time you make it you check on the absorption at around the 45-minute mark as slow cookers will vary. If there is still quite a bit of liquid, remove the lid and continue to cook, checking on it at 15-minute intervals. This can take up to 75 minutes to cook.

Toss through some coriander leaves, season with salt and pepper and serve.

# Red lentil, ginger & coriander dahl

SERVES 4–6

**D**ahl is something I started eating much later in life than I should have. And I have taken to it with a vengeance. There is something about it. It nourishes when food needs to go far beyond simply a means of sustenance to something deeper and more beautiful: food for the belly and the soul. This recipe is big on the crunch of coriander seeds, roughly crushed – I love the smokiness they add. You might get the odd bit stuck in your teeth, but it's worth it.

## Ingredients

1 teaspoon olive oil

½ onion, very finely chopped

2 garlic cloves, finely chopped

1 green chilli, deseeded and finely sliced

275 g (9½ oz) red lentils

1½ tablespoons coriander seeds, toasted
  and roughly crushed

1½ tablespoons grated ginger

1 tablespoon freshly grated turmeric

2 teaspoons Sri Lankan curry powder

1 cinnamon stick, bruised

500 ml (17 fl oz/2 cups) coconut milk

8 fresh curry leaves

## To temper

60 ml (2 fl oz/¼ cup) coconut oil

2 heaped teaspoons panch phoran

1 teaspoon brown mustard seeds

1 onion, finely sliced

1 garlic clove, crushed

2 long green chillies, finely sliced

## To serve

60 ml (2 fl oz/¼ cup) coconut cream
  (optional)

lime wedges (optional)

steamed rice

fried curry leaves (optional)

coriander (cilantro) leaves

roti (optional)

## Method

Set your slow cooker to the sauté function. Add the oil and, once hot, add the onion, garlic and chilli and cook for 1–2 minutes – just a quick fry. Add the remaining ingredients and set the heat to low. Give everything a good stir, then close the lid and cook for 2 hours.

Just before you are ready to serve, it is time to temper. Melt the coconut oil in a saucepan over a medium heat, add the panch phoran and mustard seeds, followed by the onion, garlic and chilli and fry, stirring occasionally, until the onion is tender and browned, about 5 minutes. Be careful as the seeds will spit. Remove from the heat and, when ready to serve, stir into the lentils.

Add the coconut cream and a squeeze of lime juice, if using, and season generously to taste with salt flakes.

Serve with rice, fried curry leaves, if using, coriander and roti.

# All About the Veg

**THE FOLLOWING ARE DISHES** that make their case as standalone meals, as glorious sides, or as part of a spread. Too often, the slow cooker is overlooked as a mechanism for cooking veggies, but the results are sensational. The ability of the slow cooker to retain moisture, control heat and add and build flavour, even with vegetable dishes, makes it an indispensable tool in the quest for good cooking.

# Fenugreek cauliflower curry

SERVES 4

This curry sauce is a riff on a recipe from an Indian restaurant in Canada. Originally, it was a base for lamb, but the cut-through of cauliflower is just wondrous and makes a great meat-free version for curry night. Serve it with plenty of steamed rice, naan and poppadoms.

## Ingredients

60 ml (2 fl oz/¼ cup) sweet white wine

185 g (6½ oz/¾ cup) wholegrain mustard

1 large cauliflower, broken into large
   florets (approx. 1 kg/2 lb 3 oz)

1 tablespoon rapeseed oil

## Curry sauce

1 litre (34 fl oz/4 cups) pouring (single/
   light) cream

1 tablespoon salt flakes

1 teaspoon sweet smoked paprika

½ teaspoon cayenne pepper

1 tablespoon dried fenugreek leaves

60 ml (2 fl oz/¼ cup) lemon juice

1 teaspoon ground turmeric

3 garlic cloves, crushed

## To serve

steamed rice

naan and poppadoms (optional)

coriander (cilantro) leaves

1 teaspoon panch phoran

## Method

Combine the wine, mustard, a pinch of salt and pepper and the cauliflower in a bowl. Set aside while you prepare the curry sauce.

Add the curry sauce ingredients to a large bowl and stir to combine.

Set the slow cooker to the sauté function. Add the oil and, once hot, add the cauliflower and fry for 1–2 minutes (you want to get a little colour on it). Pour over the curry sauce, close the lid and cook on low for 2 hours. You can cook this for up to 3 hours, but the cauliflower starts to lose its shape the longer it is cooked and can take on a bitter flavour. Serve with steamed rice and/or naan and poppadoms, if using, and garnish with coriander and panch phoran.

# Eggplant chreime

SERVES 4

This is a bit of a slow cooker riff on the traditional Tunisian braised fish dish of the same name. But instead, here I've cooked down eggplant in a harissa-spiced ragu and added the umami heat of urfa biber (Turkish red pepper flakes; available from specialist grocers), served on top of hummus and finished with some cooling coconut yoghurt and herbs. This one gets better with age, so embrace the leftovers.

## Ingredients

1 tablespoon olive oil

2 garlic cloves, finely sliced

2 medium eggplants (aubergines),
   trimmed, quartered lengthways

2 teaspoons cumin seeds,
   roughly crushed

1 teaspoon coriander seeds,
   roughly crushed

bunch of coriander (cilantro), roots
   trimmed, cleaned and chopped

2 ox-heart tomatoes, chopped

2 tablespoons tomato paste
   (concentrated purée)

1 × 400 g (14 oz) tin chopped tomatoes

1 tablespoon rose harissa

1 heaped teaspoon urfa biber
   (Turkish red pepper flakes)

1 tablespoon brown sugar

### To serve

150 g (5½ oz) hummus

125 g (4½ oz/½ cup) coconut yoghurt

fronds from 2 dill sprigs

chilli flakes, to taste

## Method

Preheat the slow cooker for 15 minutes on high. Set the cooker to the sauté function and add the oil, garlic, eggplant, cumin and coriander seeds. Sauté until fragrant and the eggplant starts taking on some colour. Add the remaining ingredients, give it a gentle stir, then close the lid and cook on low for 8 hours.

To serve, smear the hummus onto the base of serving plates. Gently scoop out the eggplant and place on top, then finish with the coconut yoghurt, dill and chilli flakes. Season with salt and pepper to taste.

# Cumin-braised corn, chilli, lime, coriander & feta

**SERVES 4 AS A SIDE**

The cumin adds a wonderful heat and smokiness to the corn, and I could eat this dish by the kilo. In summer I also add a lot of fresh avocado, and I promise you this is the bring-a-plate dish that will save you time and time again. If you are doubling or tripling the recipe for a bigger crowd, just fry off the corn and cumin quantities in batches so it doesn't overcrowd the bowl of your slow cooker.

## Ingredients

1 tablespoon olive oil

1 tablespoon cumin seeds, crushed

800 g (1 lb 12 oz/4 cups) fresh corn kernels
   (from about 3 large corn cobs)

zest and juice of 1 lime

250 ml (8½ fl oz/1 cup) vegetable stock

## To serve

½ bunch coriander (cilantro) leaves,
   roughly torn

1 red chilli, deseeded and finely sliced

120 g (4½ oz/½ cup) feta

fresh lime juice

## Method

Set the slow cooker to the sauté function and heat for 10 minutes or so. Add the oil and, once hot, fry the cumin seeds. Cook until fragrant, then add the corn and cook for 1 minute. Add the lime zest and juice and cook for another minute. Add the stock, then close the lid and cook on low for 1 hour. If the stock hasn't completely evaporated, turn to high, leave the lid off and watch it closely until the stock has mostly been absorbed and reduced.

Remove, season generously with salt and pepper, then turn out into a serving dish. Top with the coriander, chilli and feta and an extra squeeze of lime juice, and serve.

# Sticky spiced pomegranate beetroot

SERVES 4 AS A SIDE

T his is a spectacular way to elevate the average beetroot. I would happily eat this on its own, but it's a particularly spectacular side to lamb and chicken. Should you have any beetroot leaves on your beets, make sure you keep them. Wash them thoroughly, then fry them off in a little olive oil and add with the pistachios when serving.

## Ingredients

90 g (3 oz/¼ cup) pomegranate molasses

185 ml (6 fl oz/¾ cup) vegetable stock

1 tablespoon olive oil

2 garlic cloves, crushed

1 tablespoon chermoula spice blend

4 medium-sized beetroots, peeled
   and halved

## To serve

arils from ½ fresh pomegranate

110 g (4 oz/¾ cup) pistachio nuts,
   roughly chopped

## Method

Combine the pomegranate molasses, stock, oil, garlic and chermoula in a bowl and whisk until thoroughly incorporated.

Add the beetroot to the bowl of your slow cooker and pour over the stock mixture. Close the lid and cook on high for 1 hour. Remove the lid and check the beetroot. You want to be able to pierce it with a knife or cake tester, but have it offer some resistance as you push into the flesh. If it still seems too firm, continue to cook, checking at 15-minute intervals until tender.

Gently remove the beetroot. If you still have quite a bit of liquid in the base of your slow cooker bowl, set it to the sauté function and cook, checking at 2-minute intervals, until it has reduced further – you want about 60 ml (2 fl oz/¼ cup) left over. If you hardly have any liquid, make sure to omit this step.

Add the beetroot to a serving bowl, spoon over the remaining cooking liquid (it's okay if you don't have too much; you just want your beetroot to have a nice sticky look) and season to taste.

Scatter over the pomegranate arils and chopped pistachio nuts, and serve.

# Sweet potato with Aleppo pepper, honey & yoghurt

SERVES 4–6 AS A SIDE

Something happens to sweet potato when it is cooked this way. It becomes soft and shiny – which looks glorious on the plate – while holding its shape. And the slow, controlled cooking time only serves to intensify the potato's natural sweetness.

## Ingredients

2 tablespoons honey

½ tablespoon Aleppo pepper, plus extra
  to serve

250 ml (8½ fl oz/1 cup) vegetable or
  chicken stock

1 kg (2 lb 3 oz, about 4) small sweet
  potatoes, peeled

## Yoghurt dressing

185 g (6½ oz/¾ cup) Greek yoghurt
  (page 30)

1 garlic clove, crushed

juice of ½ lemon

## To serve

generous pinch of Kashmiri chilli powder
  (optional)

a few roughly torn mint leaves

## Method

Place the honey, Aleppo pepper and stock in a small bowl and whisk to combine.

Place the sweet potatoes in the base of your slow cooker bowl. You may need to chop them to make them fit; you want them to be rather snug and in a single layer if possible. Pour over the stock mixture and cook on low for 4 hours, then set the lid slightly ajar and cook for another 1½–2 hours.

To make the yoghurt dressing, whisk the yoghurt, garlic and lemon juice in a bowl.

Gently turn out the sweet potatoes onto a serving platter. Dollop over the dressing and add a generous pinch of Aleppo pepper, or, if you want an extra kick, the Kashmiri chilli. Scatter over the mint leaves and serve.

# Broccolini with golden raisins, tahini & sumac

SERVES 4 AS A SIDE DISH

Broccolini seems to be a vegetable that's on heavy rotation in most households – in ours, it's known as 'unicorn trees'. The raisins and tahini give a superb contrast of sweet and savoury, while the sumac and lemon keep the flavours bright. If you aren't the biggest fan of tahini, add it slowly, tasting as you go, until you are happy with the balance.

## Ingredients

½ tablespoon olive oil
2 bunches broccolini, washed
125 ml (4 fl oz/½ cup) vegetable or
  chicken stock

## Dressing

2–3 tablespoons tahini
2 tablespoons iced water, plus extra,
  if needed
juice of 1 large lemon

## To serve

30 g (1 oz/¼ cup) golden raisins or
  sultanas
generous pinch of sumac

## Method

Set the slow cooker to the sauté function. Add the oil and, once hot, add the broccolini and cook for 1 minute, turning often. The aim is to get a little bit of char without overcooking; you want to retain the shape and crunch. Add the stock, then close the lid but do not seal. You want some of the steam to escape, so use a tea towel (dish towel) to keep the lid slightly ajar. Cook for 30–45 minutes, or until the stock has mostly reduced and the broccolini is cooked but not brown and sad-looking. Season with salt and pepper.

While the broccolini is cooking, prepare the dressing. Add the tahini, water and lemon juice to a bowl and whisk to combine. If it seems too thick, thin it out with a little extra water.

When ready to serve, plate the broccolini, drizzle over the dressing, scatter over the raisins and finish with a pinch of sumac.

# Potato, leek & kale gratin with too much cheese

SERVES 4–6

This is your nan's potato bake for a new age. Because, kale. And fancy cheese. No matter how you spin it, this side dish is the ultimate wingman. Whether it's for braised meats or some crisp and bitter greens, it's a truly great culinary friend to have on hand.

## Ingredients

1 tablespoon olive oil

2 large leeks, white and light green parts only, washed thoroughly, finely sliced

½ small bunch of flat-leaf kale, stems removed, leaves chopped

375 ml (12½ fl oz/1½ cups) thickened (whipping) cream

125 ml (4 fl oz/½ cup) chicken or vegetable stock

85 g (3 oz) gruyère, grated

125 g (4½ oz) parmesan, grated

150 g (5½ oz) creamy blue cheese

900 g (2 lb) washed potatoes (I use sebago), sliced about 3 mm (¼ in) thick

## Method

Set the slow cooker to the sauté function. Add the oil and, once hot, add the leek and cook for 1–2 minutes, then add the kale and continue cooking for another 2–3 minutes, or until the leek is soft. Gently scoop into a bowl. Line the slow cooker with a sheet of baking paper, working carefully as it will be hot.

Add the cream, stock and cheeses to a bowl and use a fork to combine.

Arrange one-third of the potato slices over the bottom of the lined bowl, overlapping them slightly. Pour in one-third of the cream mixture and sprinkle with one-third of the leek mixture. Season and repeat the process until all the ingredients have been used. You should get three decent layers of cheesy potato goodness. Close the lid and cook on high for 4 hours.

Check the liquid at the 3-hour mark. If there is a lot of liquid remaining, leave the lid off for the last hour of cooking. If, at 4 hours, there is still too much liquid, remove the lid and, if your cooker has it, hit the reduce function, or simply the sauté function, and cook for 2–5 minutes. This will quickly get rid of any excess moisture.

Allow to cool for at least 15 minutes in the slow cooker before gently removing. If you try to cut it when still hot, it tends to go everywhere. Alternatively, scoop the gratin straight from the bowl onto the plate. It might not look amazing, but it's the kind of dish that is here for a good time, not a long time.

Season generously with salt and pepper and serve. Eat wearing stretchy pants; you are going to need them.

# Braised carrots with dates & coriander

### SERVES 4 AS A SIDE

You will need a large, shallow-base slow cooker for this recipe

I've found this works best with younger carrots. The smaller varieties tend to be a little sweeter and they also fit more snugly in the bowl of a slow cooker without needing to be cut. While not essential, it helps to use a slow cooker with a wider, shallow bowl so you can keep the carrots whole.

## Ingredients

250 ml (8½ fl oz/1 cup) vegetable stock

90 g (3 oz/½ cup) pitted dates,
   finely chopped

1 tablespoon coriander seeds,
   roughly crushed

500 g (1 lb 2 oz) heirloom carrots,
   washed and trimmed

## To serve

80 g (2¾ oz/¼ cup) goat's curd

coriander (cilantro) leaves

35 g (1¼ oz/¼ cup) pistachio nuts,
   roughly chopped

## Method

Combine the stock, dates and crushed coriander seeds in the bowl of your slow cooker. Add the carrots, close the lid and cook on low for 1 hour.

Gently remove the carrots, then hit the sauté function. Cook down the remaining liquid until it has reduced, about 5–10 minutes. By this stage, the dates will have broken down and the stock reduced to create a nice jammy sauce to dollop on the carrots.

Arrange the carrots on a serving platter. Scatter over the goat's curd, coriander leaves and pistachio nuts. Dollop the date sauce over the top, season with salt and pepper, and serve.

# Red curry pumpkin with typhoon shelter crumb

SERVES 4

I love this. It's rich and unctuous thanks to the curry sauce and pumpkin, then it comes alive at the end with the bam bam boom crunch of the typhoon shelter crumb.

## Ingredients

½ tablespoon rapeseed oil

1–2 tablespoons excellent-quality red
    curry paste

1 lemongrass stem, white part only, minced

800–1 kg (1 lb 12 oz–2 lb 3 oz) jap or kent
    pumpkin (squash), seeds removed, cut
    into thick wedges that will fit snugly in
    your slow cooker

1 × 400 ml (13½ fl oz) tin coconut milk

200 ml (7 fl oz) vegetable stock

1 tablespoon fish sauce

1 tablespoon palm sugar or brown sugar

juice of 1 lime

## Typhoon shelter crumb

20 g (¾ oz/¼ cup) crispy fried onion

25 g (1 oz/¼ cup) fried garlic

1 tablespoon salted peanuts,
    roughly chopped

generous pinch of chilli flakes

2 tablespoons white or black sesame seeds

2 tablespoons rice bubbles (optional)

## To serve

steamed coconut rice

coriander (cilantro) leaves, roughly torn

½ red chilli, finely sliced

3 kaffir lime leaves, deveined, finely sliced

1–2 tablespoons puffed black rice (optional)

## Method

Set the slow cooker to the sauté function. Add the oil and, once hot, add the curry paste and cook until fragrant and starting to split, about 2 minutes. Add the lemongrass and cook for another minute before adding the pumpkin pieces. Sauté briefly, until the curry mixture sticks to the pumpkin. Set the heat to low, add the remaining ingredients, then cover and cook for 4 hours. Check the pumpkin: it should be holding its shape but be soft enough to easily cut through.

While the pumpkin is cooking, combine the typhoon shelter crumb ingredients in a small bowl and set aside. Add the rice bubbles, if using.

When ready to serve, carefully scoop out the pieces of pumpkin. It will be soft, so work gently, and add to bowls of steamed rice. Top with the typhoon shelter crumb, coriander leaves, chilli, lime leaves and puffed rice, if using, then serve.

# Chermoula-stuffed leeks with goat's curd, raisins & smoked almonds

SERVES 4

You will need a
large, shallow-
base slow cooker
for this recipe

This guy here requires a pan thrown over a bit of heat to fry the leek, and I think it's worth the extra dirty dish to maximise the flavour. Caramelising part of the leeks really adds spectacular depth to the finished dish.

Use a slow cooker with a wider, flatter cooking bowl to be able to lie the leeks flat.

## Ingredients

4 leeks, trimmed, white and light green
   parts only, washed thoroughly
½ tablespoon olive oil

## Filling

zest of 1 lemon
60 g (2 oz/½ cup) sultanas (golden raisins),
   roughly chopped (or substitute with
   currants or raisins)
150 g (5½ oz) soft goat's curd
2 tablespoons chopped dill fronds
85 g (3 oz/½ cup) smoked almonds,
   roughly chopped

## Braising liquid

125 ml (4 fl oz/½ cup) white wine
125 ml (4 fl oz/¼ cup) olive oil
1 tablespoon chermoula spice blend

## Method

Cut a thin strip, about 1 cm (½ in), lengthways almost all the way through the middle of each leek (as if you were cutting a baguette). Gently pry away the strip of leek and set aside. Don't throw it out; this not only makes room for the filling but also becomes part of it. Finely chop the pulled parts of leek.

Place a frying pan over a medium heat and fry the chopped leek in the oil until soft and starting to brown in places. Remove from the heat and add to a bowl with the remaining filling ingredients, then stir to incorporate.

Line your slow cooker with baking paper so it's easier to remove the leeks once they are cooked. Place the leeks into your slow cooker dish. You want them cosy, but with enough room to splay them open and stuff with the filling. Gently press the filling along the inside of the cut leeks. Some will spill over and that is completely okay.

Combine the braising liquid ingredients in a bowl, then gently pour over the leeks. Cover and place on low heat and cook for 6 hours.

Allow to cool slightly before using the sides of the baking paper to help you gently pull the leeks from the slow cooker. Use a spatula to transfer to serving plates.

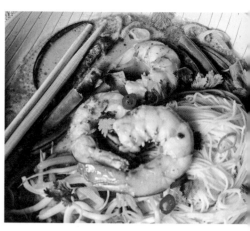

# Fragile Fridays

SOME WEEKS ARE LONG, hard and tiresome. They generally end with too much wine and talks of escaping to the countryside. Dinner, while necessary, is the last thing on our minds.

Let's face it – by the end of most weeks, things are feeling tough, but the cruellest Fridays are those that randomly turn out to be extra tricky, and for which you are totally unprepared. As an antidote to these end of week feelings, some of the recipes that follow only require you to throw a few things in the slow cooker and leave it to do its thing while you source a stiff drink. Others provide the necessary therapy of stirring, of rolling meatballs, of adding wine, and the rest fall somewhere in between.

At whichever end of the spectrum you find yourself on a Friday, there should be something here that offers comfort, solace and hopefully more than adequate gustatory satisfaction.

# Pepperoni chicken with burrata & basil

SERVES 4–6

I've amalgamated my two great pizza loves, pepperoni and margherita, and pimped them with some additional protein to help with that end-of-week energy slump.

## Ingredients

1–2 tablespoons olive oil

1 kg (2 lb 3 oz) boneless, skinless chicken thighs, cut into thirds

120 g (4½ oz) pepperoni (reserve a few slices and grill for serving)

1 red onion, chopped

1 × 400 g (14 oz) tin chopped tomatoes

250 ml (8½ fl oz/1 cup) white wine

## To serve

200 g (7 oz) ball burrata, at room temperature

1 ox-heart tomato, grated

15 g (½ oz/½ cup) basil leaves, roughly torn

crusty bread

## Method

Set your slow cooker to the sauté function. Add the oil and, once hot, add the chicken thighs and pepperoni. You may need to do this in batches to avoid overcrowding the bowl. Cook for at least 5 minutes to ensure the meat is browning and caramelising around the edges. Add the remaining ingredients, then cook for another minute. Set the temperature to low and cook for 1 hour. Taste and adjust the seasoning.

Turn out the chicken into a serving bowl and top with the burrata, grated tomato, basil leaves and grilled slices of pepperoni and serve with crusty bread on the side.

# The broken falafel: Falafel, cumin, kale & grilled haloumi with herb oil

**SERVES 4**

So, this guy you can cook overnight – in a pre-emptive strike – as a cure for end-of-week fatigue, or you can give it a quick 2 hours in the slow cooker. Whatever way you spin it, it couldn't be easier in terms of prep: you literally throw stuff in and shut the lid. Add a bit of juju with the kale and some piping hot squeaky haloumi and you're good to go.

I buy my falafels from this wonderful family at my local market. The key is the care in the making of these, so be discerning and take the time to hunt around until you find your favourite. They freeze perfectly and make for one of life's greatest last-minute snacks.

## Ingredients

750 g (1 lb 11 oz) falafel

1 × 400 g (14 oz) tin chickpeas, drained and rinsed

2 × 400 g (14 oz) tins whole tomatoes

250 ml (8½ fl oz/1 cup) vegetable or chicken stock

## Herb oil

small handful of basil leaves

60 ml (2 fl oz/¼ cup) olive oil

## To serve

8–10 cavolo nero leaves, roughly torn

8 slices haloumi

1 heaped teaspoon freshly ground cumin

## Method

Place the falafel, chickpeas, tomatoes and stock in the bowl of the slow cooker and give everything a gentle stir to combine. Close the lid and cook for 2 hours on high or set to low and cook overnight. Just before serving, add the cavolo nero leaves and allow to soften in the sauce for a few minutes.

To make the herb oil, add the basil and oil to a blender and blitz to combine, or use a hand-held blender.

When ready to serve, quickly fry the haloumi in a non-stick frying pan over a high heat. Gently scoop the falafel mixture into bowls. (Be careful because the slow cook will mean the falafels have become quite soft.) Top with slices of haloumi. Drizzle over the herb oil and sprinkle with freshly ground cumin. Taste and adjust the seasoning. Eat and forget the week that was.

# Boozy souvlaki potatoes with chorizo & feta

SERVES 4

This recipe is basically all my favourite things combined in a bowl – it's the ultimate fodder for when the soul needs feeding. Serve it with icy cold rosé or beer and it won't take long to set your personal compass back on its axis.

## Ingredients

2 fresh chorizo sausages, casings removed, meat roughly chopped

1 kg (2 lb 3 oz) white potatoes (I use sebago), washed and chopped into bite-sized chunks

1 teaspoon dried oregano

250 ml (8½ fl oz/1 cup) white wine

250 ml (8½ fl oz/1 cup) chicken stock

handful fresh oregano leaves

175 g (6 oz/1 cup) green olives, pitted

## To serve

fresh oregano leaves, roughly chopped

120 g (4½ oz/½ cup) Persian feta

fresh basil leaves, roughly torn

## Method

Set the slow cooker to the sauté function. Once hot, add the chorizo meat and cook until starting to brown and the oil is separating. Add the potato and cook for another 5 minutes, stirring gently to coat the potato in the oil. Add all the remaining ingredients, except the olives, then close the lid. Cook on high for 2 hours, then open the lid and stir through the olives to warm through.

To serve, scoop the potato mixture (and its residual liquid; there will be some) into bowls. Top with oregano, feta and basil. Season generously and serve.

# Slow-cooked zucchini & 'nduja in chardonnay

SERVES 4–6

This number tastes great and will take you a whole 5 minutes to prepare. The important part is adding the chardonnay with absolute abandon. If you don't like things too hot, pare back the 'nduja – the heat will intensify as it slow cooks. It seems like a lot of zucchini, but this breaks down and, to be honest, there is nothing wrong with the leftovers the next day.

## Ingredients

100 g (3½ oz) 'nduja sausage

1 red onion, finely chopped

6 large zucchini (courgettes), sliced
  into rounds

500 ml (17 fl oz/2 cups) chardonnay

250 ml (8½ fl oz/1 cup) chicken stock

## To serve

large pasta shells, cooked

grated parmesan

micro greens or soft herbs

## Method

Set the slow cooker to the sauté function. Once hot, add the 'nduja and onion and cook for 3–5 minutes, or until the onion is soft and the 'nduja has begun to release its oils. Add everything else, then close the lid and cook for 5 hours on low.

Cook your pasta according to the packet instructions, then add to the bowl of the slow cooker and toss everything gently to combine. Alternatively, you can serve everything separately for people to help themselves. Grate over an indecent amount of parmesan, sprinkle with the micro greens, then season generously with salt and pepper.

# Trashy ramen noodles

SERVES 2–3

I am the first to agree there is a time and place for a truly cared-for ramen – one where bits and bobs and unctuous things have intimately come together to form a perfectly crafted dish. At other times, you just want the noodles: the dodgy supermarket packet variety. Straight up. With all the funky packet spices. It's what I often imagine chefs might seek out at the end of a particularly hard and hectic service.

I saw American chef Roy Choi make his childhood instant ramen noodles adding cheese and an egg, and I was instantly hooked. He talked about it being a staple growing up and it reminded me so intensely and immediately of my mum and how she would sometimes make me a thermos of ramen noodles for school lunch on a cold day. I decided then and there that, no matter how simplistic they are, they deserved to be adapted for your slow cooker. Throw them in, leave them to do their thing, and feed everyone who needs feeding.

## Ingredients

500 ml (17 fl oz/2 cups) chicken stock

3 packets ramen noodles, plus their seasoning

3 slices pre-sliced burger or cheddar cheese

2–3 eggs, at room temperature (depending on the number of serves)

## To serve

2 tablespoons fried garlic

30 g (1 oz/¼ cup) finely sliced spring onion (scallion)

## Method

Pour the stock and 500 ml (17 fl oz/2 cups) water into the bowl of your slow cooker. Add the packets of noodles along with their seasoning. Close the lid and cook for 20 minutes on high.

Turn out the noodles and cooking liquid into bowls, and, working quickly, place a slice of cheese on top and break an egg into the side of each bowl. Using chopsticks, gently cover the egg with the noodles so that it lightly steams and cooks in the broth. Top with the fried garlic and spring onion and serve.

# Bloody Mary gnocchi with pickles & hope. And cheese. And more pickles.

SERVES 4

This recipe is for when you are done. Toast. Completely finished. If you want to pan-fry the gnocchi before throwing them in, it can add a nice touch, but not doing so certainly isn't a deal breaker.

## Ingredients

800 g (1 lb 12 oz) gnocchi

200 g (7 oz) ball mozzarella, roughly torn

### Bloody Mary mix

1 × 500 g (1 lb 2 oz) jar passata (puréed tomatoes)

100 ml (3½ fl oz) chicken stock

100 ml (3½ fl oz) celery juice

2 tablespoons dill fronds, very finely chopped

5 cm (2 in) piece horseradish, grated

60 ml (2 fl oz/¼ cup) pickle juice from a jar of pickles

2 tablespoons Worcestershire sauce

125 ml (4 fl oz/½ cup) vodka

2 tablespoons brown sugar

½ teaspoon celery salt

juice of ½ lemon

### To serve

chopped flat-leaf (Italian) parsley

mozzarella, roughly torn

spicy cucumber pickles (optional)

## Method

Combine all the Bloody Mary mix ingredients in the bowl of your slow cooker. Add the gnocchi. Shut the lid. Pour yourself a wine. Cook on low heat for 2 hours. Remove the lid, add the mozzarella, close it again and continue to cook for a further 20 minutes, or until the mozzarella has melted.

Scoop into bowls, being careful as the gnocchi will be very soft and some will break. Top with parsley, extra mozzarella and spicy pickles, if using. Serve.

# Persian meatballs in saffron & tomato sauce

SERVES 4–6

I love the hands-on therapy of rolling meatballs. The mindless monotony of the task is great for unwinding and calming a hectic mind. The rice in the meatballs ensures they stay tender and soft.

## Meatballs

500 g (1 lb 2 oz) minced (ground) lamb
100 g (3½ oz/½ cup) white rice, boiled
   until just cooked
1 garlic clove, crushed
1 egg
1 small onion, grated
½ bunch flat-leaf (Italian) parsley, leaves
   picked and finely chopped
1½ teaspoons Persian spice mix
3 dried rosebuds, petals broken (optional)

## Sauce

100 ml (3½ fl oz) olive oil, plus extra to serve
1 onion, finely chopped
10 saffron threads, crushed in
   ½ tablespoon water
2 × 400 g (14 oz) tins chopped tomatoes
200 ml (7 fl oz) wine

## To serve

1 tablespoon cumin seeds, toasted and
   roughly crushed
dried rose petals
75 g (2¾ oz/½ cup) pistachio nuts,
   roughly chopped
125 g (4½ oz/½ cup) labne
flatbreads

## Method

To make the meatballs, combine all the ingredients in a large bowl and season generously. Using your hands, roll the mix into meatballs. Aim to make them twice the size of a golf ball. Place on a baking tray or large, flat dish and refrigerate until ready to cook.

To make the sauce, set the slow cooker to the sauté function. Add the oil and, once hot, add the onion and sauté until translucent and softened. Add the saffron threads and water and cook for another minute. Add the tomatoes and wine, then close the lid and cook on high for 4 hours.

Gently drop the meatballs into the sauce, then continue cooking, uncovered, on high for an additional 30–45 minutes. This will ensure the sauce thickens and reduces a little while the meatballs cook.

Top the meatballs with a drizzle of oil and the cumin seeds. Sprinkle over the dried rose petals and chopped pistachio nuts. Serve with labne and flatbreads.

# Homely Neapolitan pasta

SERVES 4

The best bit about this dish – and other bean-based pasta dishes – is how the pasta is cooked with the vegetables and their cooking liquid, rather than in a separate saucepan of water. The starch combined with the dash of milk creates a rich, creamy sauce with zero effort on your part.

## Ingredients

2 tablespoons olive oil

1 small onion, finely chopped

1 carrot, finely chopped

2 garlic cloves, crushed

185 g (6½ oz/1 cup) laird lentils, rinsed

1 tablespoon tomato paste
  (concentrated purée)

3 lemon thyme sprigs, leaves pulled

2 bay leaves

pinch of chilli flakes

250 ml (8½ fl oz/1 cup) white wine

1 litre (34 fl oz/4 cups) vegetable stock

400 g (14 oz) short pasta, such as
  rigatoni or orecchiette

80 ml (2½ fl oz/⅓ cup) full-cream
  (whole) milk

## To serve

flat-leaf (Italian) parsley, roughly chopped

1 tablespoon lemon thyme leaves

your bodyweight in parmesan

## Method

Turn on your slow cooker while you scurry about for the ingredients. Once warmed up, set to the sauté function and add the oil. Give it 30 seconds, then add the onion, carrot and garlic. Cook for 10 minutes until soft and fragrant, then season with salt and pepper.

Add the lentils, tomato paste, lemon thyme, bay leaves and chilli flakes. Cook for another few minutes just to let the flavours meld, then add the wine and stock. Close the lid and cook on low for 3 hours, or up to 4, until the lentils are cooked through and al dente but still holding their shape. Set the cooker to high and give it 10 minutes to come up to the right heat, then add the pasta and milk and cook for 20–25 minutes. Discard the bay leaves.

Divide the pasta between serving bowls and garnish with the herbs and glorious amounts of cheese.

# Rose harissa salmon biryani, or kedgeree of sorts

SERVES 2–3

I cooked this for 45 minutes and it's the perfect balance between cooking the grains and not overcooking the fish. I suggest trying this with your slow cooker and adapting the cooking time accordingly. When I tried for pinker fish, the rice still had too much bite, as did the onion, so for me, 45 minutes kept everything in balance.

It's the ultimate shove-in-and-forget dish while you find the wine and the remote.

## Ingredients

1 tablespoon olive oil

1 onion, finely chopped

1 tablespoon coriander seeds,
  roughly ground

1 teaspoon toasted cumin seeds,
  roughly ground

2 teaspoons rose harissa, or to taste

100 g (3½ oz/½ cup) basmati rice

95 g (3¼ oz/½ cup) Israeli couscous

435 ml (15 fl oz/1¾ cups) vegetable stock

400 g (14 oz) skinless salmon fillets

## To serve

coriander (cilantro) leaves, roughly
  chopped

## Method

Set the slow cooker to the sauté function. Add the oil and, once hot, add the onion, ground coriander and cumin seeds. Sauté for 3–5 minutes, or until the onion has started to soften. Add the harissa, rice and couscous, and cook for another 30–60 seconds. You want the grains coated in the mixture, as if you were cooking a risotto.

Add the stock and give everything a good stir. Turn the heat to low, gently place the salmon fillets on top, close the lid and cook for 45 minutes. Check the salmon at the 35–40-minute mark. If it is too pink for you, continue to cook, checking on it every 1–2 minutes until cooked to your liking. Scatter over the coriander, season, and serve.

# Slow cooker laksa

SERVES 2–3

I use a shop-bought laksa paste. Quelle horreur! But with a few in-the-pan additions, you can elevate a decent-quality paste into something very closely resembling those spectacular Malaysian-inspired bowls of pure, soul-restoring goodness. The key is to not dump the paste straight in with a tin of coconut milk – you need to build layers of flavour. Depending on the brand, the laksa paste's heat and intensity of flavour can vary, so use the amounts given here as a guide.

## Ingredients

1 tablespoon rapeseed oil

3 garlic cloves, crushed

5 cm (2 in) piece ginger, grated on a mandoline

1 lemongrass stem, white part only, bruised then grated on a mandoline

2 red chillies, finely sliced (deseeded if desired)

55–115 g (2–4 oz/¼–½ cup) laksa paste

1 × 400 ml (13½ fl oz) tin coconut milk

375 ml (12½ fl oz/1½ cups) chicken stock

2 teaspoons fish sauce

juice of 1 lime, plus extra to season

6–8 prawns (shrimp), peeled, deveined, tails intact

100 g (3½ oz/1 cup) vermicelli noodles, softened in boiling water

## To serve

90 g (3 oz/1 cup) bean sprouts

150 g (5½ oz/1 cup) green beans, trimmed and chopped into bite-sized pieces

coriander (cilantro) leaves, to garnish

## Method

Set your slow cooker to the sauté function. Add the oil and, once hot, add the garlic and ginger and sauté for 30–45 seconds until fragrant, then add the lemongrass and the sliced chillies. Continue to cook for another minute. Add the laksa paste and cook, stirring constantly, until fragrant and it looks like it is beginning to split. Turn the heat to low. Stir in the coconut milk, stock, fish sauce and lime juice. Close the lid and cook for 1 hour.

Remove the lid and turn the heat to high. Add the prawns and cook for 2–3 minutes, or until just cooked through. Gently remove and, working quickly, pour the laksa into serving bowls. Add the rice noodles and top with the prawns, the bean sprouts, beans, and coriander. Season with extra lime juice and serve piping hot.

# Cheat's green curry slurpy dumplings

SERVES 2

This one is for the truly fragile; it's a mere list of ingredients that require little more than assembly. The key to making it sing? A decent curry paste and the best dumplings you can find.

## Ingredients

2 teaspoons excellent-quality green
  curry paste
1 × 400 ml (13½ fl oz) tin coconut milk
1 teaspoon fish sauce
1 teaspoon white sugar
300 g (10½ oz) fresh or frozen dumplings
  (I use chicken and Chinese cabbage/
  wombok; see Note)
70 g (2½ oz/½ cup) shelled edamame
80 g (2¾ oz/½ cup) freshly podded peas

## To serve

zest and juice of 1 lime
fresh herbs, to scatter (coriander/cilantro,
  Thai basil and mint work well)
Chinese black vinegar

## Method

Add the curry paste to the bowl of your slow cooker. Set to the sauté function and cook for about 45–60 seconds, or until the paste is fragrant and looks as though it is about to split. Add the coconut milk, fish sauce and sugar. Stir to combine, then add the dumplings and close the lid. Set the cooker to low heat and cook for 45 minutes, then add the edamame and peas. Cook for a further 5 minutes.

  Gently scoop into bowls and season with the lime zest and juice. Add the fresh herbs and drizzle over black vinegar to taste. Put on your stretchy pants. Slurp at will.

**Note** / If you use fresh instead of frozen dumplings, you will need to reduce the cooking time by approximately half.

# Freezer Fodder

**IN A PICTURE-PERFECT ORGANISED** life, I'd have a freezer full of slow-cooked goodness that I could draw upon at a moment's notice. There I'd be, swanning around my kitchen, gin in hand, while the chaos rained down around me. This is rarely a reality, but I can say, hand on heart, that on the few occasions I have actually managed to double-batch a meal to shove on ice, it has saved my skin and my sanity.

These recipes are for eating now, or eating later, or a combination of the two. Everything freezes well, but I strongly advise you label your lovingly prepared dish before it gets lost in the recesses of your freezer. You might think you'll remember what that Tupperware container is hiding, but you won't. Promise. And then, one night, you'll be looking forward to curry only to be greeted with tacos, and that's the kind of disappointment no one needs (though tacos are always delicious).

The following recipes can easily be doubled to maximise your one-for-now, one-for-later options, or you can simply cook, cool and freeze.

# Tandoori white beans with mint & coriander relish

SERVES 6

eans freeze like a dream, making this one essential for your freezer stash. My one piece of advice? Don't forget the salt. It performs some funky alchemy between the sodium ions and the cells of the bean skin, making sure they keep their glorious shape throughout the longer cooking time.

The first time you cook this, I suggest you check on it around the 5-hour mark to see if it needs any more liquid – just a splash of stock should do it. Give it a stir, then leave it well alone.

If you are concerned about the lectin in dried beans, see page 15 for preparation instructions.

## Ingredients

700 g (1 lb 9 oz) dried white beans

### Relish

1 small bunch coriander (cilantro) leaves

½ small bunch mint leaves

½ small onion, diced

2 garlic cloves, chopped

1 teaspoon finely grated ginger

1 teaspoon Kashmiri chilli powder

1 tablespoon lemon juice

1 teaspoon cumin seeds, toasted

### Braising liquid

1 tablespoon finely grated ginger

1 tablespoon finely chopped garlic

1 tablespoon tandoori paste

½ tablespoon ground cumin

½ tablespoon ground coriander

1 teaspoon garam masala

½ teaspoon ground turmeric

500 ml (17 fl oz/2 cups) vegetable stock, plus extra if needed

### To serve

coriander (cilantro) leaves

mint leaves

200 g (7 oz) Yoghurt (optional; page 30)

naan or roti

## Method

For the relish, add all the ingredients to a blender and blitz to combine. You still want some texture, so don't overwork it; you're looking for a chunky pesto style rather than a sauce. Cover and pop in the fridge until you are ready to use it.

Rinse your beans thoroughly, then add to the bowl of your slow cooker with the braising liquid ingredients and a generous pinch of salt. Give everything a good stir, then close the lid and cook on low for 8–10 hours. If the beans seem a little too thick, add more stock or water to loosen.

Plate the tandoori beans and top with the green relish, extra coriander, mint and yoghurt. Serve with naan.

# Wagyu beef korma

SERVES 6–8 AS PART OF A SPREAD

Ask your butcher for some wagyu offcuts (they often have cuts out the back that didn't make it to their display cabinets and that you can usually buy for a song). For a more wallet-friendly version, you can simply substitute with good old chuck steak.

This dish is spectacular as part of a spread with the Butter chickpeas on page 127 and the Indian-spiced sweet potato with tomato & cream on page 133.

## Ingredients

175 ml (6 fl oz) ghee

3 onions, finely diced

1 kg (2 lb 3 oz) wagyu beef, cut into
  large chunks

4 cm (1½ in) piece ginger, grated

2 garlic cloves, chopped

1 red chilli, deseeded, minced
  (or 1 teaspoon excellent-quality
  chilli paste)

2 pinches ground turmeric

1 tablespoon ground coriander

1 tablespoon garam masala

300 g (10½ oz) Yoghurt (page 30)

450 ml (15 fl oz) beef stock

## To serve

sliced green chilli

coriander (cilantro) leaves

fried garlic

small handful flash-fried curry leaves

cooked rice or naan

poppadoms

lime cheeks

## Method

Set your slow cooker to the sauté function. Add the ghee and, once hot, fry the onion until translucent. You want to get it as soft as possible. Don't rush this step; this is where a lot of the flavour for this curry base comes from. Give it at least 10 minutes cooking time, stirring regularly. Add the meat, ginger, garlic, chilli, turmeric, coriander and garam masala to the bowl. Season with salt and pepper. Stir constantly, moving the meat and spices in and around the onion mixture, for up to 5 minutes. Depending on the size of your slow cooker, you may need to do this in batches. Add the yoghurt and then the stock, close the lid and cook on low for 10 hours.

Garnish with the chilli, coriander, fried garlic and curry leaves, and serve with rice, poppadoms, fresh lime and your favourite choice of sides.

# Chicken, kale & feta dumplings with Sicilian olives

SERVES 4–6

This is glorious. The flavour of the olives infuses the tomato sauce during the low and slow cook, and yet this dish still feels light enough to serve with some simple greens or grains in summer, or in front of a fire with fresh, thick-cut fettuccine and a glass of red in winter. Regardless of the season, there are a few key things to note. Try to find young, fresh leaves of kale; they are less bitter and you don't have to worry about removing the stems before you chop. Secondly, visit a butcher – I always ask for my chicken to be freshly minced. I've found a 50:50 balance of breast and thigh works like a dream.

## Ingredients

500 g (1 lb 2 oz) minced (ground) chicken

120 g (4½ oz/½ cup) Persian feta

1 red onion, finely chopped

1½ teaspoons sweet smoked paprika

2 garlic cloves, crushed

4 large leaves flat-leaf kale, very
  finely sliced

1 tablespoon olive oil

175 g (6 oz/1 cup) Sicilian olives, pitted

1 × 400 g (14 oz) tin crushed tomatoes

310 ml (10½ fl oz/1¼ cups) white wine

½ tablespoon brown sugar

2 tablespoons tomato paste
  (concentrated purée)

## To serve

roughly chopped flat-leaf (Italian) parsley

baby kale leaves

## Method

Add the chicken, feta, onion, paprika, garlic and kale to a bowl. Using your hands, work the mixture until the ingredients are thoroughly incorporated, then roll into large, golf ball–sized meatballs.

Set your slow cooker to the sauté function. Add the oil and, once hot, gently add the meatballs and cook until lightly browned, turning occasionally. Add the olives, crushed tomatoes, wine, brown sugar and tomato paste. Close the lid and cook on low for 8 hours.

Season generously with salt and pepper before serving. If you're using extra kale leaves to serve, simply push them into the hot sauce to soften just before serving. Scatter with the baby kale to finish.

### Ideas for accompaniments

- Israeli couscous
- Herby rice pilaf
- Fresh, thick-cut fettuccine (and a wonderful, full-bodied pinot)

# Overnight black-eyed pea tacos with mezcal, cotija & grilled corn salsa

SERVES 4

You really need to start with dried beans, not tinned, for this to work. If you use tinned beans the whole thing turns into a gloopy mess, but with the dried beans, it's a spicy, textural wonderland and well worth the (minimal) extra work.

If you are concerned about the lectin in dried beans, see page 15 for preparation instructions.

## Ingredients

400 g (14 oz/2 cups) black-eyed peas, rinsed

2 × 400 g (14 oz) tins crushed tomatoes

250 ml (8½ fl oz/1 cup) vegetable or chicken stock

2 teaspoons chipotle in adobo, chopped

1½ teaspoons freshly ground cumin

1 teaspoon sweet smoky paprika

1½ teaspoons ground coriander

1 cinnamon stick

2 tablespoons roughly chopped oregano leaves

1 garlic clove, crushed

1 onion, coarsely grated

2 teaspoons brown sugar

## Mezcal, cotija & grilled corn salsa

5 g (⅛ oz) butter

2 small corn cobs, kernels removed

1 tablespoon mezcal

60 g (2 oz/¼ cup) cotija cheese (substitute with feta if unavailable)

## Cheat's chipotle mayo (optional)

125 g (4½ oz/½ cup) Kewpie mayonnaise

1 heaped teaspoon chipotle powder, or to taste

## To serve

corn or mini flour tortillas

shredded red cabbage

coriander (cilantro) leaves, roughly chopped

vegetable or edible flowers (optional)

lime cheeks

## Method

Add all the black-eyed pea ingredients to the bowl of your slow cooker and stir to combine. Cook on low for 8 hours until the peas are tender, then season generously with salt.

To make the salsa, melt the butter in a frying pan over a medium heat. Add the corn kernels and cook, tossing regularly, for 1 minute, or until the corn is starting to colour. Add the mezcal and cook until the liquid has mostly evaporated. Tip into a bowl with the cheese and toss to combine.

To make the chipotle mayo, whisk the ingredients with a fork in a small bowl to combine.

Warm the tortillas according to the packet instructions. Serve the beans in the tortillas topped with the corn salsa, mayo, if using, cabbage and coriander and vegetable flowers, if using, with lime cheeks on the side.

# XO, ginger & pineapple-braised beef short ribs

SERVES 4–6

You'll need a nice big slow cooker for this number – all the bones take up a lot of room. It also needs an early start, as the 12-hour cook really allows the unctuous goodness of these ribs to come through.

Because the meat-to-bone ratio can vary when you buy beef short ribs from the butcher, assess the amount of liquid in the slow cooker once the ribs are in. If it seems that a lot of the ribs aren't covered by the sauce, just add another 125 ml (4 fl oz/½ cup) or so of stock. You can also check on this after a few hours, as once the meat starts to break down you will be able to push the meat and bones down a bit to better submerge them in the liquid.

**You will need a large-volume slow cooker for this recipe**

## Ingredients

1 tablespoon coconut oil

1 small red onion, finely chopped

3 large garlic cloves, crushed

1 tablespoon freshly grated ginger

2 teaspoons curry powder

2 kg (4 lb 6 oz) beef short ribs

2½ tablespoons tomato paste (concentrated purée)

80 ml (2½ fl oz/⅓ cup) soy sauce

1 tablespoon apple-cider vinegar

80 ml (2½ fl oz/⅓ cup) XO sauce

375 ml (12½ fl oz/1½ cups) pineapple juice

2 tablespoons palm sugar

125 ml (4 fl oz/½ cup) master stock

125 ml (4 fl oz/½ cup) ginger beer

## To serve

cooked rice noodles

Thai basil leaves

Vietnamese mint leaves

coriander (cilantro) leaves

1 red chilli, halved lengthways, deseeded and finely sliced

80 g (2¾ oz/½ cup) crushed peanuts

toasted coconut flakes

lime wedges

## Method

Set your slow cooker to the sauté function. Once hot, add the coconut oil and allow to melt and warm up. Add the onion and cook until fragrant, about 3–5 minutes. Add the garlic, ginger and curry powder and cook, stirring regularly to prevent them catching, for about 1 minute. Add the ribs and cook, trying to brown on each side. (Depending on the size of your slow cooker bowl, you may need to do this in batches.) Once browned, add the remaining ingredients and allow the mixture to come to a bit of a rolling boil on high, then turn the heat down to low, close the lid and cook for 12 hours.

Allow the mixture to cool slightly, then gently pull the bones from the meat. Using a couple of forks, gently shred the meat and return it to the sauce. Leave the lid off and turn the heat to high while you prepare the rice noodles and toppings. This will allow the sauce to reduce and thicken slightly. If you think it has reduced sufficiently already, just skip this step.

Serve the noodles topped with the beef rib mixture, fresh herbs, chilli, nuts and coconut, and some lime on the side.

Freeze any leftover rib mixture for another use. It's great served over steamed rice or as a filling in a rice paper roll with some crunchy salad.

# Lemongrass & basil chicken in coconut curry sauce

SERVES 6

I f you are using a shop-bought lemongrass paste over fresh, double the quantity of lemongrass below to ensure the flavour carries through.

## Ingredients

1 tablespoon coconut oil

1 onion, finely chopped

6 garlic cloves, crushed

2 tablespoons finely chopped lemongrass

2 tablespoons dried basil

small handful of basil leaves, finely
    chopped

½ tablespoon grated ginger

1 kg (2 lb 3 oz) boneless, skinless chicken
    thighs, cut into thirds

2 tablespoons yellow curry powder

pinch of chilli powder

1 × 400 ml (13½ fl oz) tin coconut milk

## To serve

steamed coconut rice

salted peanuts

Thai basil leaves

Vietnamese mint leaves

coriander (cilantro) leaves

lime wedges

roti (optional)

## Method

Set the slow cooker to the sauté function and add the coconut oil. Once hot, add the onion and cook for 3–5 minutes, or until fragrant and softened. Add the garlic, lemongrass, basil and ginger, and cook, stirring frequently, for another 1–2 minutes, or until fragrant.

Add the chicken in batches – being careful not to overcrowd the bowl of the slow cooker; you don't want it to sweat – and cook until all the chicken has been browned. Return the chicken to the bowl and add the curry and chilli powders and a generous seasoning of salt and pepper. Add the coconut milk, give everything a good stir, then close the lid and cook on low for 8 hours. At the end of the cooking time, remove the lid and set on high – or use the reduce function on your slow cooker if you have one – and reduce for 10 minutes to thicken the sauce slightly. Depending on the rate of evaporation, you may not even need to do this step.

Serve with steamed rice, peanuts, herbs, fresh lime and piping hot roti.

# Butter chickpeas

SERVES 4–6

If you are feeling virtuous, feel free to substitute coconut milk for the coconut cream – it will just have a thinner consistency. But, honestly, if we are going for those takeaway-style vibes, just add the coconut cream. Life is short. And it tastes amazing.

If you are concerned about the lectin in dried beans, see page 15 for preparation instructions.

## Ingredients

½ tablespoon coconut oil

1 large red onion, finely chopped

1 heaped tablespoon grated ginger

3 garlic cloves, crushed

1 cinnamon stick

2 teaspoons each of sweet smoked paprika and ground cumin

1 teaspoon each of fennel seeds, ground fenugreek and ground coriander

1 tablespoon garam masala

225 g (8 oz) dried chickpeas

1 × 400 g (14 oz) tin crushed tomatoes

1 × 400 ml (13½ fl oz) tin coconut cream

125 ml (4 fl oz/½ cup) vegetable stock

100 g (3½ oz) butter

1 teaspoon brown sugar (if needed)

## To serve

saffron rice

coriander (cilantro) leaves, chopped

naan or poppadoms

Yoghurt (page 30)

pickles (optional)

lime cheeks

curry leaves (optional)

## Method

Set the slow cooker to the sauté function and add the coconut oil. Once hot, add the onion, ginger, garlic and spices. Stir constantly with a wooden spoon to prevent the spices from catching. Once fragrant, add the chickpeas, crushed tomatoes, coconut cream, stock and butter. Close the lid and cook on high for 4 hours.

Season with salt. The bitterness of tinned tomatoes can vary considerably, so taste and add the brown sugar if the sauce tastes slightly bitter. Keep tasting and seasoning until you feel you have the right balance of flavours.

Serve with rice, coriander and all the good stuff: naan, poppadoms, yoghurt, pickles and fresh lime. I love to flash-fry a few fresh curry leaves and stir these through the rice, but if you don't have the time or inclination, feel free to omit.

# The ultimate chilli chicken

SERVES 6

Normally, I specify browning your meat and aromatics first when it comes to slow cooking, but this recipe is a dump-and-run scenario. It builds on layers, starting with the chicken and, for whatever reason, it just works.

I wanted a chilli chicken that wasn't tomato based, and this is it. Given the variation between slow cookers, liquid can evaporate at different speeds, so I have included an option for thickening the sauce. This is by no means mandatory – just make sure you shred the chicken into the sauce before you decide if it needs thickening (it will absorb more liquid when shredded).

Even though it's called chilli chicken, this dish is mild. When slow cooking, you can really intensify the heat, so it's best to incorporate the fire of a good chilli at the end – with chilli flakes, fresh green chilli, whatever you like. The last thing you want to do is make it so hot that it is inedible, and you find you have wasted all those great ingredients.

If you can't find masa flour, you can substitute with half cornmeal and half plain (all-purpose) flour, and if you are concerned about the lectin in dried beans, see page 15 for preparation instructions.

## Ingredients

4 skinless chicken breasts (approx. 1 kg/2 lb 3 oz)
1 tablespoon each ground cumin and ground coriander
2 teaspoons dried oregano
1 tablespoon finely chopped fresh oregano
1 teaspoon sweet smoked paprika
2 teaspoons chipotle powder
200 g (7 oz/1 cup) dried white beans, washed thoroughly
2 celery stalks, sliced
4 garlic cloves, minced
3 jalapeño chillies, deseeded and finely chopped
1 onion, chopped
2 green capsicums (bell peppers), deseeded, chopped
1 litre (34 fl oz/4 cups) chicken stock
zest and juice of 1 lime
60 g (2 oz/½ cup) grated Monterey Jack cheese (or use cheddar/feta if unavailable)

### Optional thickener

185 ml (6 fl oz/¾ cup) full-cream (whole) milk
40 g (1½ oz/¼ cup) masa flour (see intro)

### To serve

extra cheese, if desired
sour cream
coriander (cilantro) leaves and oregano
corn tortillas or tortilla chips
sliced green chilli
chilli flakes
avocado, diced

## Method

Place the chicken breasts in the base of the slow cooker. Mix the cumin, coriander, oregano (dried and fresh), paprika and chipotle in a bowl, then sprinkle over the chicken, tossing evenly to coat. Top with the remaining ingredients, except the lime zest and juice and cheese, then close the lid and cook on low for 10 hours.

Using a couple of forks, gently shred the chicken in the bowl of your slow cooker and stir it through the sauce. If, at this point, you feel the sauce needs thickening, mix the milk with the masa flour, pour into the slow cooker and stir to combine. Close the lid and cook on low for another 10–15 minutes, or until the sauce has thickened.

Add the lime zest and juice and adjust the seasoning with salt and pepper. I love to add cheese straight to the pot before serving and stir it through the chicken so that it melts. Serve with all the extras.

# Sausage ragu with ricotta & spelt pasta

SERVES 6–8

I 'll often double this one up and keep a permanent stash of it on rotation. It freezes like a dream and has got me out of many a last-minute dinner scrape, particularly when friends drop in for a drink and then decide to stay for the evening. I have used spelt pasta in this recipe, but any pasta will do.

## Ingredients

1 tablespoon olive oil

2 onions, finely chopped

2 garlic cloves, chopped

1 large carrot, finely chopped

1 celery stalk, finely sliced

1 large rosemary sprig, leaves picked

1 large lemon thyme sprig, leaves pulled

1 kg (2 lb 3 oz) excellent-quality beef sausages, casings removed, meat roughly chopped

3 tablespoons tomato paste (concentrated purée)

250 ml (8½ fl oz/1 cup) dry white wine

2 × 400 g (14 oz) tins chopped tomatoes

75 g (2¾ oz/½ cup) smoked semi-dried tomatoes, roughly chopped

600 g (1 lb 5 oz) pasta

## To serve

flat-leaf (Italian) parsley and basil leaves, chopped

35 g (1¼ oz/¼ cup) smoked semi-dried tomatoes, to scatter

250 g (9 oz/1 cup) excellent-quality ricotta

40 g (1½ oz/¼ cup) pitted black olives, halved, to scatter (optional)

## Method

Set your slow cooker to the sauté function. Add the oil and, once hot, add the onion and cook for 2–5 minutes, or until soft. Add the garlic, carrot and celery and cook for another 10 minutes, or until the vegetables have softened considerably. Add the herbs and cook for another 30 seconds before adding the sausage meat. Cook for 5–8 minutes, or until the meat is beginning to brown and caramelise. Don't rush this step; it's important for the meat to take on quite a bit of colour for added flavour. Add the tomato paste, wine, chopped tomatoes and semi-dried tomatoes. Set the slow cooker to low, close the lid and cook for 10 hours. Season generously.

Cook the pasta according to the packet instructions. Drain and serve topped with the sausage ragu, fresh herbs, semi-dried tomatoes, ricotta, olives, if using, a drizzle of oil and some freshly ground black pepper.

# Indian-spiced sweet potato with tomato & cream

SERVES 6

You can easily double or triple this recipe and freeze portions for all those curry-in-a-hurry requirements down the track. It is nothing short of wondrous served with piping hot naan, some steamed rice and some quick-sautéed spinach. I even recommend blitzing the dregs, the leftover sauce and broken-down bits of pumpkin in a blender and enjoying it as a glorious soup.

## Ingredients

2 tablespoons coconut oil
1 red onion, finely chopped
1 teaspoon salt flakes
4 garlic cloves, crushed
2½ tablespoons finely
 grated ginger
1 tablespoon garam masala
2 teaspoons cumin seeds,
 toasted and ground
1 teaspoon panch phoran
2 teaspoons ground turmeric
½ tablespoon coriander
 seeds, toasted and ground
½ teaspoon sweet smoked
 paprika
¼ teaspoon Kashmiri chilli
 powder
1 teaspoon ground cardamom
2 tablespoons tomato paste
 (concentrated purée)
1 kg (2 lb 3 oz) sweet potato,
 peeled and cut into large
 pieces

## Broth

1 × 400 g (14 oz) tin crushed
 tomatoes
250 ml (8½ fl oz/1 cup)
 pouring (single/light) cream
500 ml (17 fl oz/2 cups)
 vegetable stock

## To serve

drizzle of coconut cream
1 teaspoon panch phoran,
 flash-fried in hot oil
coriander (cilantro) leaves,
 roughly torn

## Method

Set your slow cooker to the sauté function. Add the coconut oil and, once hot, add the onion and cook for 2–5 minutes, or until soft and fragrant. Add the salt and garlic and cook for another minute before adding the ginger and all the spices. Cook briefly, until the onion mixture is coated in the spices and becomes fragrant, about 1–2 minutes. Add the tomato paste and cook for 1 minute. (The mixture should take on a thicker consistency.)

Add the sweet potato and cook for another minute, stirring regularly so the pieces are coated in the onion and spice mixture. Next, add the broth ingredients, give everything a good stir to combine, then close the lid and cook for 6 hours on low.

Turn out into serving bowls, being gentle as the sweet potato will be soft, and drizzle with coconut cream. Top with the flash-fried panch phoran and coriander leaves to serve.

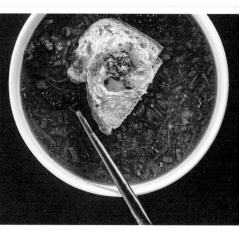

# Soup
# Kitchen

**I'VE NEVER FORGOTTEN A** particularly austere German chef in culinary school who tasted my soup – a very simple potato soup. Evidently, I had perfected the roundness of flavour: I had sweated the onions into oblivion and countered their sweetness with an appropriate level of seasoning. But top marks would not be mine; my soup was, she said with a sigh, 'far too Australian'. Obviously, Australians make their soup too thick. Who knew? I have no idea if this is even a thing? Maybe it is, but it hasn't stopped me. I love a chunky soup, one that I can stand a piece of toast in, scatter with an array of toppings that won't sink to the bottom, and wipe up the dregs with a piece of piping hot roti. So be warned: the following soups may differ in origin, but they do carry that hallmark 'Australian' thickness. And I'm not even sorry.

# Easy Mexican tortilla soup

SERVES 4

This couldn't be easier, or more comforting, on those overcast, stay-at-home-and-potter kind of days. You could also pop this on low for 8 hours while you are at work for a soul-restoring mid-week meal.

## Ingredients

2 tablespoons olive oil

1 onion, finely chopped

2 garlic cloves, minced or grated

1 tablespoon chipotle in adobo, chopped, sauce reserved

1 teaspoon coriander seeds, toasted and roughly crushed

2 teaspoons cumin seeds, roughly crushed

1 teaspoon dried oregano

1 teaspoon sweet smoked paprika

2 × 400 g (14 oz) tins crushed tomatoes

250 ml (8½ fl oz/1 cup) vegetable or chicken stock

1 × 400 g (14 oz) tin black beans, drained and rinsed

zest and juice of 1 lime

## To serve

sliced avocado

tortilla chips

shredded Monterey Jack cheese (or cheddar or crumbled feta if unavailable)

chopped coriander (cilantro) leaves

## Method

Set the slow cooker to the sauté function. Add the oil and, once shimmering, add the onion and garlic. Cook for 3–5 minutes, or until fragrant and soft. Add the chipotle in adobo and the spices. Cook for another minute, stirring to coat the onion. Add all the remaining ingredients, except for the lime zest and juice, and give it a good stir. Close the lid and cook for 4 hours on high, or 8 hours on low.

Season with the lime zest and juice, and some salt and pepper. Ladle into bowls and top with sliced avocado, tortilla chips, cheese and chopped coriander. Serve piping hot.

# Lasagne soup

SERVES 6

This is a bit of a win for the workdays. Pop it on in the morning; it doesn't matter if it cooks for 6 hours or 10. When you get home, you simply add the lasagne sheets and cook for 20–30 minutes and dinner is done. It has a place at the table on any old Wednesday night as much as it does on the nights you have friends over for dinner. It is a feat of comfort and culinary genius all in one. Looking at those lasagne sheets bobbing happily in the soupy, cheesy sauce is a feast for the eyes as well as the belly.

## Ingredients

2 tablespoons olive oil

1 onion, finely chopped

3 garlic cloves, crushed

1 celery stalk, finely chopped

1 carrot, finely chopped

1 teaspoon dried oregano

1 tablespoon finely chopped oregano
   leaves

1 tablespoon finely chopped basil leaves

500 g (1 lb 2 oz) minced (ground) beef

185 ml (6 fl oz/¾ cup) full-cream
   (whole) milk

2 × 400 g (14 oz) tins chopped tomatoes

500 ml (17 fl oz/2 cups) chicken stock

2 tablespoons tomato paste
   (concentrated purée)

100 g (3½ oz/1 cup) grated parmesan

200 g (7 oz) fresh lasagne sheets,
   roughly torn

1 ball buffalo mozzarella, roughly torn

### To serve

basil leaves

## Method

Set the slow cooker to the sauté function and allow to warm up. Add the oil and, once hot, add the onion. Cook for 1–2 minutes, then add the garlic, celery and carrot. Cook for 2 minutes, stirring regularly to prevent them catching. Add the herbs and cook for another 30 seconds before adding the beef. Cook until lightly browned, then season with salt and pepper.

Stir in the milk and cook for another 5 minutes, or until it looks like the milk has been absorbed into the meat and none of the meat is clumping together. Add the tomatoes, stock and tomato paste, then close the lid and cook on low for 6–8 hours. Lift the lid and add half of the parmesan to season. Once melted into the sauce, gently push in the lasagne sheets. Close the lid and cook for 30 minutes. Turn off the heat. Add the mozzarella and give it a minute to melt into the sauce. Gently spoon into serving bowls. Season again with the remaining parmesan, salt and pepper and add the fresh basil leaves just before serving.

# Roasted lemon chicken & burghul yoghurt soup with chilli oil

SERVES 4 GENEROUSLY

L ife is for living, so feel free to substitute the roasted chicken for barbecued chook. It's a very worthy stand-in when time and the inclination to cook are at a low.

## Chicken

1 large chicken breast, on the bone,
  skin on
½ tablespoon olive oil
1 teaspoon dried mint
1 lemon, zested (zest reserved, see
  Grains section below), then sliced

## Grains

2 tablespoons olive oil
300 g (10½ oz) coarse burghul
  (bulgur wheat), rinsed
zest of 1 lemon (see above)
250 ml (8½ fl oz/1 cup) chicken stock,
  or as required
200 g (7 oz/1 cup) cooked basmati rice
1 garlic clove, crushed
½ bunch flat-leaf (Italian) parsley,
  finely chopped

## Soup

500 ml (17 fl oz/2 cups) chicken stock
1 kg (2 lb 3 oz/4 cups) Greek yoghurt
  (page 30)
1 egg
1 tablespoon cornflour (cornstarch)
1 teaspoon dried mint

## To serve

1 teaspoon chilli sauce/hot sauce
1 tablespoon olive oil
strips of lemon zest

## Method

Preheat the oven to 180°C (350°F).

Cover the chicken breast with the oil and rub in the mint. Cover with the lemon slices. Place on a roasting tray lined with baking paper and roast for 20 minutes, or until cooked. You can check by inserting a skewer into the thickest part of the breast to make sure the liquid runs clear. Using a few forks, shred the meat, skin and lemon into a bowl. Pop in the fridge while you cook the grains.

To prepare the grains, set your slow cooker to the sauté function. Add the oil and, once hot, add the burghul and lemon zest and cook, stirring regularly, until the burghul begins to colour and has a nutty aroma. Add just enough stock to cover the grains, then set the heat to low and cook for 45 minutes. You don't want the grains to turn into a gloopy mess, so be sparing with your stock — it should only just cover the burghul.

Add the burghul to the bowl of shredded chicken, along with the rice, garlic and parsley, and stir to combine. Season generously.

To finish the soup, return the bowl of the slow cooker to the unit, add the stock and yoghurt and turn the heat to low. The key here is warming it through gently so the yoghurt doesn't curdle. If it has a warming function, you could just set it to this and warm it nice and slowly. Cook for about 15 minutes, then add the egg and sift over the cornflour, stirring continuously until fully incorporated. Once it looks as though it has thickened slightly, it is ready to go. Stir through the dried mint and season generously with salt and pepper.

To serve, combine the hot sauce and olive oil in a bowl and mix well. Divide the chicken and burghul mixture between bowls. Carefully ladle the soup over the top and spoon over some of the chilli oil. Add the strips of lemon zest and serve immediately.

# Old school 12-hour tomato soup

SERVES 6

No one seems to make tomato soup anymore. I can never find it on a menu. There are old favourites dressed up in all manner of disguises (hey there, pumpkin) and a plethora of broths and phos, but it's hard to find a really great tomato soup. So, here is one: a wonderful combination of tomato, fennel and a dash of paprika. Serve it with cheese toasties – it would be criminal not to.

This soup also freezes well and can be rolled out for use in different dishes: as a base for pasta sauce or for smearing over your pizza bases. It really is a gift that keeps on giving.

## Ingredients

60 ml (2 fl oz/¼ cup) olive oil

45 g (1½ oz) butter

2 red onions, sliced

1 fennel bulb, finely sliced

2 teaspoons sweet smoked paprika

1½ teaspoons coriander seeds, lightly
   crushed

1 teaspoon fennel seeds, lightly crushed

3 × 400 g (14 oz) tins chopped tomatoes

250 ml (8½ fl oz/1 cup) vegetable or
   chicken stock

3 teaspoons brown sugar, plus extra
   if needed

## To serve

thickened (whipping) cream or Yoghurt
   (optional; page 30)

grilled cheese toasties

## Method

Set your slow cooker to the sauté function. Add the oil and butter and, when hot, add the onion and sliced fennel with a big pinch of salt. Cook, stirring often to prevent the vegetables catching, until they have softened and started to sweat. Add the paprika, coriander and fennel seeds and cook for 10–12 minutes, or until the vegetables are very soft. You may need to nurse this phase a little; you don't want the spices to burn, but you do want the onion mixture to be thoroughly coated in the spices, and for it to be nice and fragrant. Add the tomatoes, stock and sugar. Close the lid and cook on low for 10–12 hours.

Allow the soup to cool slightly in the pot before using a hand-held blender to blitz it. Taste and adjust the seasoning with salt and sugar as needed. (Depending on your tomatoes, the soup can taste a little acidic and will need the additional sugar and salt to temper it.)

Pour the soup into serving bowls. Drizzle with cream or yoghurt, if using, and season again. Serve with cheese toasties.

# Spicy rendang lentil soup

SERVES 4 GENEROUSLY

I know rendang and lentils may at first seem at odds. After all, they probably aren't two ingredients you would think to combine, but it just works. Trust me. I've included a recipe for the rendang paste here. I feel it's really worth making your own, often in a double batch, then freezing the rest for later, but at a pinch you can substitute with a quality shop-bought version if your blender or your motivation are broken.

## Rendang paste

6 red chillies, roughly chopped (seeds removed if you want to reduce the heat)

6 garlic cloves, roughly chopped

7 cm (2¾ in) piece ginger, roughly chopped

2 red onions, roughly chopped

125 ml (4 fl oz/½ cup) melted coconut oil

1 tablespoon Malaysian curry powder

90 g (3 oz/1 cup) shredded coconut, toasted

6 fresh curry leaves

1 tablespoon sweet smoked paprika

½ teaspoon ground cinnamon

½ teaspoon ground coriander

1 tablespoon brown sugar

juice of 1 lime

1 lemongrass stem, white part only, roughly chopped

## Soup

1 × 400 ml (13½ fl oz) tin coconut cream or milk, reserving 1 tablespoon for drizzling

600 ml (20½ fl oz) vegetable or chicken stock

150 g (5½ oz) red lentils, rinsed and drained

1 × 400 g (14 oz) tin chopped tomatoes

2 tablespoons coriander (cilantro) leaves and stalks, washed and finely chopped

## To serve

lime wedges

coriander (cilantro) leaves, chopped

## Method

Put the rendang paste ingredients in a blender and blitz to a coarse paste. Ensure the fibrous strands of lemongrass have been properly macerated in the paste. Reserve half the paste in the fridge for another use.

Set your slow cooker to the sauté function. Once hot, add the paste and cook until fragrant and starting to split. Add the coconut cream and cook until it looks like it has split. Add the stock and cook for a further minute, or until warmed through. Add the lentils, chopped tomatoes and coriander leaves and stalks. Close the lid and cook on low for 4 hours, or until the lentils are broken down and soft but the soup still has some texture.

Ladle into bowls and drizzle with the reserved coconut cream and a squeeze of lime juice. Scatter over a few extra coriander leaves and serve piping hot.

See image on page 16.

# Prawn tom yum

SERVES 4

I love a tom yum – the kind that has that fragrant, nose-clearing heat and just enough chilli to cause a sheen across your forehead and a tingle on your lips.

The broth requires a little bit of work, but to get that glorious, clear, fragrant stuff, you do have to dirty a few extra dishes.

If you leave out the prawns, mushrooms and tomato from the base broth, this is very freezer friendly. You can thaw the broth and add these elements at the end.

## Ingredients

1 litre (34 fl oz/4 cups) chicken stock
1 ox-heart tomato, cut into wedges
½ onion, cut into small wedges
2 teaspoons caster (superfine) sugar
3 tablespoons fish sauce
zest and juice of 1 lime
500 g (1 lb 2 oz) prawns (shrimp), peeled and deveined
4–6 oyster mushrooms, roughly torn

### Tom yum paste

2 vine-ripened tomatoes, roughly chopped
20 g (¾ oz) each of ginger and galangal, roughly chopped
6 kaffir lime leaves, roughly torn
4 garlic cloves, roughly chopped
4 coriander (cilantro) stalks, roots scrubbed
3 red shallots, roughly chopped
2 red bird's eye chillies, roughly chopped
2 lemongrass stems, white part only, finely sliced
2 tablespoons brown sugar

### To serve

bird's eye chilli, sliced
coriander (cilantro) leaves
kaffir lime leaves, deveined, finely sliced

## Method

To make the paste, add all the ingredients to a food processor and blitz to combine.

Set your slow cooker to the sauté function and, once hot, add the paste. Cook very briefly, about 1 minute, then add the stock. Change the setting to high and bring to the boil, then turn the heat to low and allow the flavours to infuse for 45 minutes.

Strain into a bowl, wipe the bowl of your slow cooker and return it to the unit. Set it to high and return the soup to the bowl. Add the tomato, onion, sugar, fish sauce and lime zest and juice, then stir to combine. Add the prawns and mushrooms and cook, lid off, for another 60–90 seconds, or until the prawns have just cooked through. Ladle into bowls and top with extra sliced chilli, fresh coriander and sliced kaffir lime leaves.

# Spicy pearl barley soup
# with hidden meatballs

SERVES 6

O h, how I love this soup. It's so chunky and thick, crossing the divide between soup and stew, just the way I like it. You will be hard-pressed to find something more comforting or nourishing. The sliced black garlic adds the most delightful, funky sweetness – just the little oomph this soup needs.

## Hidden meatballs

400 g (14 oz) minced (ground) beef

1 onion, grated

1 tablespoon flat-leaf (Italian) parsley, finely chopped

1 tablespoon coriander (cilantro) leaves, finely chopped

1 teaspoon ground cumin

1 teaspoon ground coriander

½ teaspoon ground allspice

## Soup

2 tablespoons olive oil

1 onion, finely chopped

2 garlic cloves, chopped

2 carrots, finely sliced

2 celery stalks, finely sliced

1 tablespoon Baharat spice mix

1 tablespoon ground coriander

1 tablespoon ground cumin

1 tablespoon caster (superfine) sugar

1 tablespoon tomato paste
 (concentrated purée)

165 g (6 oz/¾ cup) pearl barley

1 litre (34 fl oz/4 cups) chicken or
 vegetable stock

1 × 400 g (14 oz) tin chopped tomatoes

## To serve

2–3 black garlic cloves, finely sliced

flat-leaf (Italian) parsley, roughly chopped

## Method

For the meatballs, combine all the ingredients in a bowl until well mixed. Roll the mixture into small meatballs – you should get about 18. Pop in the fridge while you prepare the soup base.

Add the oil to the bowl of the slow cooker and set to the sauté function. When warm, add the onion, garlic, carrot and celery and cook for 5 minutes, or until softened. Add the spices and sugar, and cook for another minute before adding the tomato paste. Stir to coat, then add the meatballs. The bowl will be crowded so push the carrot and onion mixture to the side and lightly brown the meatballs for a few minutes. Add the pearl barley and stock and tomatoes and stir gently to combine. Close the lid and cook for 4 hours on high.

Season generously with salt and pepper. Pour into serving bowls and serve piping hot topped with sliced black garlic and parsley.

# Crisper zuppa

SERVES 4–6

So, the list of ingredients below is only a guide; this soup exists for using up leftovers. That is how the Italians run with it, and how you should too. The pasta added at the end makes it gloriously starchy and a bit thick and luscious. A squeeze of lemon juice to finish never hurt anyone, either. Often, sausage and cream are also added, but here, I've kept it packed full of veg, and it is just as flavoursome.

## Ingredients

2 tablespoons olive oil

2 onions, chopped

2 garlic cloves, crushed

4 carrots, sliced

2 waxy potatoes, chopped

2 celery stalks, finely chopped

4–6 leaves cavolo nero,
   roughly chopped

4 zucchini (courgettes), sliced

3 tablespoons tomato paste
   (concentrated purée)

handful flat-leaf (Italian) parsley,
   chopped

500 ml (17 fl oz/2 cups) white wine

500 ml (17 fl oz/2 cups) vegetable stock

180 g (6½ oz/2 cups) short pasta
   (ziti works well, as it can handle the
   longer cook)

## To serve

shaved parmesan

pinch of chilli flakes (optional)

## Method

Set the slow cooker to the sauté function. Add the oil and, when hot, add the onion, garlic, carrot, potato, celery, cavolo nero and zucchini and cook for at least 10 minutes, stirring until fragrant and the zucchini looks soft. Add the tomato paste and parsley and stir to coat. Next, add the wine and stock and give everything a good stir. Season, then close the lid and cook on low for 6–8 hours.

Add the pasta and cook for another hour. Check it at this point, as it may need a little longer. When the pasta is cooked, pour the soup into bowls. Top with salt and pepper and a generous amount of shaved parmesan and chilli flakes, if using.

# Sort of French onion miso soup

**SERVES 4–6**

I secretly adore French onion soup, but think it could do with a little more funk and salty umami flavour. Enter miso paste and oyster sauce: they add brilliant background flavours to this classic. Just don't forget the cheese toastie finisher; it's not the same without it.

## Ingredients

3 tablespoons olive oil

8 small onions, finely sliced

8 garlic cloves, crushed

185 ml (6 fl oz/¾ cup) white wine

750 ml (25½ fl oz/3 cups) vegetable stock

2 tablespoons oyster sauce

1 tablespoon white miso

## To serve

finely snipped chives

freshly ground black pepper

grilled cheese toasties (always)

## Method

Set the slow cooker to the sauté function. Add the oil and, when hot, add the onion and cook, stirring often, for 8–10 minutes, or until softened and beginning to sweat. Don't rush this part; you want that glorious, subtle caramelisation to occur. Add the garlic and cook for another minute before adding the wine, stock and oyster sauce. Give everything a good stir, then close the lid and cook for 8 hours on low. Just before serving, stir through the miso and cook for a further 10 minutes, then check for seasoning.

To serve, ladle the soup into bowls. Scatter with chives and season with pepper. Serve with grilled cheese toasties.

See image on page 134, top right.

# Ash–e–reshteh Persian noodle soup

**SERVES 6**

I wish I had discovered the glory of this Persian soup earlier in life. It is chock-full of herbs, beans, lentils and noodles, and is the sort of soul-restoring soup that takes care of your wellbeing in every sense. I'm not going to lie: to make it truly amazing, you need all the toppings – the yoghurt, the mint oil, the fried onions and the saffron water. Then, the glory is all yours.

If you are concerned about the lectin in dried beans, see page 15 for preparation instructions.

## Ingredients

2 litres (68 fl oz/8 cups) vegetable stock

100 g (3½ oz/½ cup) dried white beans

45 g (1½ oz/¼ cup) dried green or brown lentils

55 g (2 oz/¼ cup) dried chickpeas

200 g (7 oz) dried noodles, (you may find reshteh/thin noodles in Persian/Iranian grocery stores, or you can use linguine)

30 g (1 oz/½ cup) finely sliced spring onion (scallion), white part only

250 g (9 oz/5 cups) chopped spinach

1 small bunch finely chopped flat-leaf (Italian) parsley

1 tablespoon finely chopped mint leaves

## Mint oil

60 ml (2 fl oz/¼ cup) rapeseed oil

2 tablespoons dried mint

## Saffron water

pinch of crushed saffron threads

2 tablespoons boiling water

## Fried onion (optional)

½ tablespoon olive oil

1 onion, finely chopped

1 teaspoon ground turmeric

## To serve

garlic chips (optional)

Yoghurt (page 30)

## Method

For the mint oil, add the oil to a small saucepan and place over a medium heat. Swirl to coat the pan, stir through the dried mint and remove from the heat. Set aside until ready to serve.

Combine the stock, beans, lentils and chickpeas in the bowl of your slow cooker. Close the lid and cook on low for 8 hours. Add the noodles and turn the heat to high. Cook for 8–12 minutes, or until al dente. Turn the heat off, then add the spring onion, spinach and herbs, stirring gently to combine. Leave to sit – the greens will soften in the residual heat while you quickly prepare the toppings.

Combine the saffron and boiling water in a small bowl, cover and let sit.

For the fried onion, if using, place all the ingredients in a frying pan over a medium heat and cook until soft and golden, about 10 minutes. Using a slotted spoon, transfer the onion to a bowl.

Taste the soup and adjust the seasoning as needed, then divide between bowls. Garnish with the fried onion and garlic chips, if using, yoghurt, mint oil and saffron water, and serve.

# Weekend Wanderlust

**PRE-CHILDREN, BRUNCH** was something I lived for. Now I can only dream of those long, idle mornings spent somewhere spectacular, be it at a restaurant, at my best friend's kitchen bench or on a blanket in the park with a group of friends or family. I loved the languid hours spent eating and chatting, eating and drinking. Then doing it on repeat. I also loved the fluidity – it seems to be the only meal where dessert is a perfectly acceptable way to start, verge away from, then return to.

Life seems to get in the way of this most relaxing meal, so here is a little bit of inspiration and motivation for bringing it back: the beauty of long days spent with some of your favourite people with some glorious food to boot.

# Overnight loaded pumpkin shakshuka

**SERVES 6**

The addition of pumpkin is a win here, sort of like it has always belonged. And if ever there was a versatile brunch dish, this is it. If you need to bulk it out, try stirring through some Israeli couscous and some roughly torn cavolo nero.

## Ingredients

60 ml (2 fl oz/¼ cup) olive oil

1 red onion, finely sliced

3 garlic cloves, crushed

800 g (1 lb 12 oz) jap or kent pumpkin (squash), peeled, cut into medium–large chunks

220 g (8 oz/1 cup) finely sliced piquillo peppers (roasted peppers)

1 bay leaf

1 teaspoon cumin seeds, toasted and roughly crushed

½ teaspoon rose harissa

1 × 400 g (14 oz) tin cherry tomatoes

200 ml (7 fl oz) vegetable stock

140 g (5 oz) tomato paste (concentrated purée)

## To serve

6 eggs

120 g (4½ oz/½ cup) Persian feta

mint leaves

coriander (cilantro) leaves, chopped

½ tablespoon urfa biber (Turkish red pepper flakes)

## Method

Set your slow cooker to the sauté function. Add the oil and, once hot, add the onion and garlic and cook for 3–5 minutes, or until softened. Add the pumpkin, piquillo peppers and spices. Cook until fragrant, about another minute. Add the rose harissa, cherry tomatoes, stock and tomato paste. Give it a good stir, then turn the heat to low, close the lid and cook for 10–12 hours.

When you are ready to serve, crack the eggs directly into the spicy stew and sprinkle over chunks of feta. Cover and cook on high for 12–15 minutes, or until you can see the egg whites are setting but the yolks are still soft. The timing for this may vary, so keep a close eye on it. Scatter over the herbs and urfa biber to serve.

# Eggs in isolation
# with zhoug

SERVES 4–8

This is a riff on an Ottolenghi recipe with the added zing of zhoug. Calling this purely breakfast is somewhat limiting, as I think it would also make a rather spectacular meal at any other time of day.

## Ingredients

8 eggs, at room temperature

100 ml (3½ fl oz) rapeseed oil, or other flavourless oil

1 onion, finely chopped

1 tablespoon coriander seeds, toasted and roughly crushed

1 teaspoon caraway seeds, toasted and roughly crushed

1 teaspoon cumin seeds, toasted and lightly crushed

1½ tablespoons tomato paste (concentrated purée)

3 garlic cloves, crushed

3 teaspoons urfa biber (Turkish red pepper flakes)

1 × 400 g (14 oz) tin crushed tomatoes

## Zhoug

1 teaspoon caraway seeds

2–3 long green chillies, roughly chopped (deseeded if desired)

3 garlic cloves, crushed

1 teaspoon ground cardamom

½ teaspoon ground cloves

1 bunch coriander (cilantro) leaves

60 ml (2 fl oz/¼ cup) olive oil

1½ teaspoons lemon juice

## To serve

120 g (4½ oz/½ cup) Persian feta

crushed pistachio nuts

coriander (cilantro) leaves

## Method

Half-fill a large saucepan with water and bring to the boil. Turn down the heat to medium so the water is boiling gently, then lower in the eggs and cook for 6 minutes. Drain, then place the eggs under cold running water for a few minutes to stop the cooking process. Gently peel and refrigerate until serving.

Set your slow cooker to the sauté function and add the oil. Once hot, add the onion and cook until softened, then add the coriander, caraway, cumin, tomato paste, garlic and a pinch of salt, and cook for 2 minutes, stirring occasionally, until aromatic. Add the urfa biber and tomatoes, stir to combine, then close the lid and cook on low for 1 hour. If you want to you can cook these down for longer, just loosen the tomato mixture with stock or more tomatoes and continue cooking for up to 4 hours.

While the tomato mixture is cooking, prepare the zhoug. Dry-toast the caraway seeds in a frying pan over a medium–high heat until fragrant, then coarsely crush with a mortar and pestle. Add the chilli, garlic, cardamom and cloves, season to taste and pound until broken down, about 1–2 minutes. Add the coriander leaves and half the oil and pound to break down the leaves, about 30 seconds, then stir in the lemon juice and remaining oil and season to taste.

When you are ready to serve, give the tomato mixture a quick blitz with a hand-held blender. This is completely optional and if you prefer to leave it chunkier and more rustic, omit this step. Gently add the eggs to the tomato mixture, and continue to cook with the lid off for up to 5 minutes, or until the eggs have completely warmed through. You can also just bring the eggs to room temperature and serve on top of the tomato mixture if you prefer.

Spoon into serving bowls and drizzle over the zhoug. Scatter over a few pieces of feta, the crushed pistachio nuts and coriander, then serve.

# Quick apple-pie oats with fresh fruit

SERVES 2–4

This is a quick(ish) and super creamy version of oats – not quite porridge, but not quite bircher; something sitting in between the two that can be eaten warm, straight from the bowl of leftovers, or cold from the fridge.

## Ingredients

125 g (4½ oz/1 cup) rolled (porridge) oats

375 ml (12½ fl oz/1½ cups) apple purée

375 ml (12½ fl oz/1½ cups) full-cream (whole) milk

2 tablespoons milk powder

35 g (1¼ oz/½ cup) dried apple pieces, chopped

1 teaspoon ground cinnamon

1 teaspoon mixed spice

¼ teaspoon ground cloves

3 teaspoons vanilla bean paste

250 g (9 oz/1 cup) Greek yoghurt (if needed; page 30)

185 ml (6 fl oz/¾ cup) apple juice (if needed)

1 green tart apple, grated

## To serve

pinch of ground cinnamon

Greek yoghurt (page 30)

fresh seasonal fruit

fresh honeycomb (optional)

freeze-dried fruits (optional)

## Method

Set your slow cooker to low. Add all the ingredients, except the yoghurt, apple juice and grated apple. Season with a pinch of salt and give everything a good stir to combine. Cook for 40 minutes. Give the oats another stir and loosen with the yoghurt and apple juice, if required.

Stir through the grated apple before adding to serving bowls. Top with a pinch of cinnamon, more yoghurt, fruit and fresh honeycomb and freeze-dried fruits, if using.

# Strawberry & pink peppercorn crumble bars

SERVES 4–8

I love making something like this using the slow cooker instead of a traditional oven as there is no danger of the fruit mixture burning, which often happens in the oven depending on the level of sugar in the fruit and jam.

If you are desperate for that crunchy browned top, you can finish these in the oven for 10 minutes, but that classifies as unnecessary effort in my book.

I found I had a bit of leftover base mixture by the time I had sprinkled it over the fruit, so rather than scale back the quantity, I have left it as is. The extra mixture is handy in case your fruit is quite wet and you need some extra topping to absorb moisture, or if you like an extra-thick base. Or if, like me, you decide to make a few quick oat cookies. Simply add a bit more melted butter, roll into balls and bake.

You will need a 22 cm (8¾ in) springform cake tin to make this recipe. Don't use frozen fruit; it is too wet for slow cooker conditions and won't work.

## Base

250 g (9 oz/2 cups) rolled (porridge) oats
150 g (5½ oz/1 cup) plain (all-purpose) flour
140 g (5 oz/¾ cup, lightly packed)
  brown sugar
200 g (7 oz) unsalted butter, melted,
  plus extra for greasing

## Strawberry filling

375 g (13 oz/2½ cups) strawberries,
  hulled and halved
1½ teaspoons pink peppercorns,
  lightly crushed
1 tablespoon brown sugar
2 teaspoons vanilla bean paste
160 g (5½ oz/½ cup) strawberry jam

## To serve

crushed freeze-dried strawberries
½ tablespoon pink peppercorns,
  to scatter

## Method

Grease and line a 22 cm (8¾ in) springform cake tin.

Add the rolled oats to a food processor and blitz to a flour-like consistency.

Add the remaining base ingredients with a pinch of salt and blitz to combine. Press a generous amount across the base of the cake tin and slightly up the side. Set aside the remaining mixture for the topping.

Set your slow cooker to high. Make a sling for the base of the cake using aluminium foil or baking paper. This will make it a lot easier to remove the cake from the bowl at the end. Lay the sling inside the bowl, then pop the cake tin on top and cook with the lid off for 1 hour. The base won't take on colour as such, but it will cook and harden like a biscuit.

While the base is cooking, combine the filling ingredients in a bowl and stir to fully incorporate the vanilla and peppercorns. Spoon the mixture over the base, then sprinkle over chunks of the remaining oat mixture — much like a crumble — being rather generous as this will meld into the fruit as it cooks. Cook for another hour, or up to 2 hours depending on how soft the fruit is. You really don't have to oversee this at all as it can't burn, but you do want the fruit to cook through and break down a little with the jam. Using the sling, remove the cake tin from the cooker, allow to cool slightly, then pop in the fridge for a few hours to firm up.

Leftover pieces are best stored in the fridge for up to 1 week.

# Muesli

MAKES APPROXIMATELY 1 KG (2 LB 3 OZ/6–8 CUPS)

I was a complete disbeliever that muesli could be prepared in a slow cooker, until of course, I tried it. This little mini oven toasts the oats on low heat to glorious effect. Just make sure you leave the lid ajar, or if you have a slow cooker that seals, leave the lid open completely and throw a tea towel (dish towel) over the top, covering about three-quarters of the bowl for evenly toasted perfection. And the best bit? The coconut oil roasting away makes your house smell like the beach, and probably that much-needed tropical holiday.

## Ingredients

375 g (13 oz/3 cups) rolled (porridge) oats

70 g (2½ oz/2 cups) puffed rice or spelt

15 g (½ oz/½ cup) puffed quinoa

1 tablespoon vanilla bean paste

125 ml (4 fl oz/½ cup) melted coconut oil

80 ml (2½ fl oz/⅓ cup) maple syrup

370 g (13 oz/2 cups) mixed dried fruit

25 g (1 oz/¼ cup) shredded coconut

15 g (½ oz/½ cup) yoghurt drops

## Method

Set your slow cooker to high. Add the oats, puffed rice and quinoa, vanilla, coconut oil and maple syrup to the bowl and use a wooden spoon to toss everything until well coated. Cook, with the lid ajar, for 2 hours. Stir once or twice when walking past.

Spread out on a tray to allow the mixture to cool completely, then add to a bowl with the dried fruit, coconut and yoghurt drops and toss to combine before storing in airtight containers for up to 2 weeks.

# Dulce de leche croissant bread & butter bake with honeycomb

SERVES 4–6

I've always felt good about blurring the line between breakfast and dessert. It's the culinary equivalent of keeping the lines of communication open, and this dish is a great example.

I tend to leave the lid off this one; I like the croissant tops to maintain a bit of crispness. You can also pop the slow cooker bowl under the grill (broiler) at the end for a few minutes to crisp up the tops.

This tends to work best in a slow cooker with a wide dish so the croissants can be placed in a single layer.

**You will need a large, shallow-base slow cooker for this recipe**

## Ingredients

100 g (3½ oz) Dulce de leche (page 28)

6 small croissants, halved

## Batter

300 ml (10 fl oz) pouring (single/light) cream

100 ml (3½ fl oz) full-cream (whole) milk

2 teaspoons vanilla bean paste

90 g (3 oz) caster (superfine) sugar

3 eggs

1 egg yolk

## To serve

175 g (6 oz/½ cup) Dulce de leche (page 28)

50 g (1¾ oz/1 cup) honeycomb pieces, roughly broken

80 g (2¾ oz/½ cup) roasted macadamia nuts, roughly chopped (optional)

## Method

Spread the dulce de leche over the base half of each croissant, then gently sandwich the croissants together.

Line your slow cooker with baking paper, making sure you have quite a bit of paper running up the sides so that it is easy for you to remove the pudding at the end. Gently layer the croissants across the base of the slow cooker bowl, adjusting to fit as snugly as possible. Turn your slow cooker to the low setting.

Combine the batter ingredients in a jug and gently pour between the croissants. Try to avoid pouring the batter over the tops of the croissants – you want to ensure they stay nice and crispy. Cook on low, with the lid off, for 1½ hours. The time here will vary between slow cookers, but the easiest way to check if the pudding is cooked is to touch the egg mixture in a few spots – it should spring back.

When it feels cooked, drizzle over more dulce de leche. If you want to get your croissant tops nice and crispy, remove the bowl and place it under the grill (broiler) for 1 minute, ensuring that the caramel doesn't burn.

Serve generous spoons of pudding with additional dulce de leche on the side, and topped with chunks of honeycomb and roasted macadamias, if using.

# Kale & mushroom strata

SERVES 6

You will need a large, shallow-base slow cooker for this recipe

This is, essentially, your omelette on toast without having to get your frying pan to the perfect temperature, and the cooked mushrooms make for a wonderful surprise. It's ideal for feeding a crowd, or you can simply halve the recipe below and make it a rather generous serving for two.

Cooking the eggs like this gives them the most glorious, custard-like mouthfeel. I'll never use a regular oven for this style of cooking ever again.

This tends to work best in a slow cooker with a wide dish so that some chunks of bread stay firm while others soften.

## Ingredients

2 tablespoons olive oil

30 g (1 oz) butter

½ onion, finely chopped

225 g (8 oz) mixed mushrooms

2 tablespoons marjoram or
    lemon thyme leaves

200 g (7 oz/4 cups) cubed, day-old
    sourdough (crusts on)

150 g (5½ oz/2 cups) chopped
    cavolo nero

6 eggs

250 ml (8½ fl oz/1 cup) full-cream
    (whole) milk

250 ml (8½ fl oz/1 cup) pouring
    (single/light) cream

75 g (2¾ oz/½ cup) grated mozzarella

75 g (2¾ oz/½ cup) grated Swiss cheese

1 teaspoon dijon mustard

## To serve

flash-fried saltbush leaves (optional)

## Method

Set the slow cooker to the sauté function. Add the oil and butter and, once the butter is melted and foaming, add the onion and cook for 3 minutes, or until starting to soften. Add the mushrooms and herbs and turn the heat to low. Cook for 15 minutes, or until the mushrooms are beginning to soften.

Gently remove the mushroom mixture and wipe out the bowl of your cooker, then line it with some baking paper. Add the bread chunks and mushroom mixture (reserving one or two bigger mushrooms for the top), then add the cavolo nero and toss gently to combine. Nestle the reserved mushrooms on top.

Add the eggs, milk, cream, cheeses and mustard to a jug and whisk to combine. Pour over the bread mixture, then cook on low for 1½–2 hours. I keep the lid off, but if you prefer to keep it on, line the lid with a paper towel to capture the moisture.

Scoop into bowls and season generously with salt and pepper. Top with saltbush leaves, if using.

# Low 'n' slow chipotle tomato beans with prosciutto crumb

SERVES 4–6

A ll good and decent breakfast spreads deserve some slow-cooked beans. Nothing is more miraculous with toast and eggs, coffee and a slab of avocado. It's what slow weekends are made of. These also freeze very well should you find yourself with leftovers.

If you are concerned about the lectin in dried beans, see page 15 for preparation instructions.

## Ingredients

1 tablespoon olive oil

1 onion, finely chopped

7 garlic cloves, crushed

2 teaspoons cumin seeds, toasted
   and ground

2 bay leaves

1 cinnamon stick

1 chipotle chilli in adobo, chopped

2 tablespoons brown sugar

2 tablespoons apple-cider vinegar

3 tablespoons tomato paste
   (concentrated purée)

200 g (7 oz/1 cup) dried cannellini beans
   (or other white bean), washed thoroughly

750 ml (25½ fl oz/3 cups) vegetable or
   chicken stock

200 g (7 oz) tinned chopped tomatoes

## Prosciutto crumb

4 slices prosciutto

1 teaspoon balsamic glaze

2 slices sourdough, blitzed to a
   rough crumb

olive oil, for drizzling

## To serve

fresh avocado

Yoghurt (page 30) or sour cream (optional)

coriander (cilantro) leaves, roughly
   chopped

## Method

Set the slow cooker to the sauté function. Add the oil and, when hot, add the onion and cook for 3–5 minutes, or until soft. Add the garlic, cumin, bay leaves and cinnamon and cook for a further 1–2 minutes. Add the chipotle in adobo, the brown sugar, vinegar and tomato paste. Cook for another minute before adding the beans and stirring to coat. Pour over the stock and tomatoes, close the lid and set the heat to low. Cook for 10 hours, or overnight.

You want the beans to be pliable and the liquid to have reduced to a thick and rich sauce. Remove the bay leaves and cinnamon before serving.

Just before serving, prepare the prosciutto crumb. Preheat the oven to 180°C (350°F). Place the prosciutto slices on a baking tray lined with baking paper and drizzle over the balsamic glaze. Pop in the oven for 10 minutes, or until the prosciutto looks dark and golden. Remove and allow to cool, then blitz to a rough crumb in a food processor. Combine with the breadcrumbs, a drizzle of olive oil and a generous amount of salt and pepper.

Serve bowls of beans topped with the prosciutto crumb, a chunk of avocado and the yoghurt or sour cream, if using, and garnish with coriander.

# California dreaming sausage & egg breakfast burritos

SERVES 4

This has got to be the ultimate meal for the day-after-the-night-before kind of scenario. I adore this with and without the cheese; the slow cooker does the most wondrous, silky things to the slow-cooked egg mixture that is otherworldly, and sometimes (only sometimes) the cheese can just be an unnecessary distraction.

## Ingredients

½ tablespoon olive oil

1 onion, finely chopped

2 beef sausages, casings removed, meat chopped

1 mild chorizo sausage or mildly spiced sausage, casing removed, meat chopped

1 teaspoon coriander seeds, ground

1 teaspoon cumin seeds, ground

6 small floury potatoes, chopped into bite-sized pieces

6 large eggs

170 ml (5½ fl oz/⅔ cup) pouring (single/light) cream

1 teaspoon chipotle powder

2 spring onions (scallions), white part only, finely chopped

60 g (2 oz/½ cup) shredded cheddar cheese (optional)

## To serve

coriander (cilantro) leaves

fresh tortillas

## Method

Set your slow cooker to the sauté function. Add the oil and, once hot, add the onion, sausage meats and spices and cook for 5 minutes, or until browned. Add the potato and continue cooking until the meat is browned and the potato is coated in the juices. It will also begin to soften, about 10 minutes.

Combine the eggs, cream, chipotle powder and spring onion in a bowl and whisk to combine. Gently pour over the sausage mixture, then set the heat to low. Cook for 45–60 minutes, then sprinkle over the cheese, if using. Leave the lid off and cook for a further 5 minutes, or until the cheese has melted.

Season with salt and pepper, then scoop the mixture into fresh, hot tortillas and top with coriander leaves to serve.

# Steeped fruits extravaganza

MAKES APPROXIMATELY 325 G (11½ OZ)

I t's my inner nanna: I just love a bit of soft, steeped fruit. It is such an easy thing to throw together and supplies me with breakfast beyond the weekend and into a busy week. Whether it's with yoghurt, blended as part of a smoothie, on muesli or on its own, it is one of the most useful fridge staples.

## Ingredients

175 g (6 oz/½ cup) honey

2 tablespoons rosewater

2 cinnamon sticks

zest of 2 oranges

3 teaspoons vanilla bean paste

## Fruit mix

75 g (2¾ oz/½ cup) dried apricots

40 g (1½ oz/½ cup) dried peaches

40 g (1½ oz/½ cup) dried apples

40 g (1½ oz/½ cup) dried pears

70 g (2½ oz/½ cup) medjool dates, pitted

70 g (2½ oz/½ cup) prunes

## Method

Set the slow cooker to high. Combine all the ingredients with 750 ml (25½ fl oz/3 cups) water in the bowl of the slow cooker and cook, with the lid off, until the honey has dissolved and everything is well combined. Continue to cook for about 30 minutes to allow the liquid to reduce by about half. Add the fruit mix, close the lid and turn the slow cooker off. The residual heat will soften and rehydrate the fruit, but prevent it from turning to mush.

Allow to cool completely in the syrup – at least 45 minutes – before storing in a sealed container in the fridge for up to 1 week.

# A Wee Bit Fancy

**SOMETIMES IT IS REALLY** lovely to make a bit of fuss and bother about dinner: to plan a meal, buy the ingredients and enjoy a quiet potter in the kitchen getting everything ready. It's such a beautiful contrast to those 'just getting through it' moments when dinner is yet another item to cross off the list. So, the following recipes are for exactly that: when you want to put a little bit of care and attention into the meal you're preparing.

# Sichuan braised eggplant

SERVES 2, OR 4–6 AS PART OF A SPREAD

Traditionally, this is made with some pork mince added to the mix, but I love it as a vegetarian option and quite like to serve it with crispy fried tofu and steamed rice on the side. It is dead easy to make – nothing actually fancy about it, other than the taste – which is nothing short of glorious, and it is something I imagine you would share as part of a spread of delicious dishes to gorge on banquet style.

## Ingredients

2 tablespoons rapeseed oil

1 large eggplant (aubergine), cut into
   large cubes

5 black garlic cloves, sliced

8 cm (3¼ in) piece ginger, sliced and
   chopped finely

½ tablespoon roughly crushed
   Sichuan peppercorns

1 tablespoon brown sugar

2 tablespoons soy sauce

1 tablespoon Chinese black vinegar

80 ml (2½ fl oz/⅓ cup) vegetable or
   chicken stock

1 teaspoon chilli bean paste

### To serve

freshly snipped chives

steamed rice

flash-fried firm tofu (optional)

## Method

Set your slow cooker to the sauté function. Add the oil and, once hot, cook the eggplant in batches, turning regularly until starting to brown on the edges and soften, about 5 minutes. Add the garlic and ginger and cook for another minute until fragrant. Add the remaining ingredients, stir to coat, then turn the slow cooker to low. Close the lid and cook for 1 hour.

Gently turn the eggplant mixture out into a serving plate and top with the chives. Serve piping hot with steamed rice and some flash-fried tofu, if using.

# Mushroom ragu with gnocchi

SERVES 4

The unctuous, six-hour cooked mushrooms in this dish show that a ragu doesn't have to be all about meat. This is so completely indulgent and luxurious. Serve with quickly pan-fried gnocchi or fresh pappardelle and superb-quality parmesan or pecorino.

## Ingredients

60 g (2 oz) butter

1½ tablespoons olive oil

1 onion, finely chopped

6 garlic cloves, crushed

1 kg (2 lb 3 oz) mixed mushrooms
(such as Swiss, oyster, portobello,
enoki), roughly chopped

2 teaspoons marjoram leaves,
finely chopped

2 teaspoons lemon thyme leaves,
finely chopped

250 ml (8½ fl oz/1 cup) white wine

250 ml (8½ fl oz/1 cup) vegetable,
mushroom or veal stock

## To serve

gnocchi or pappardelle

zest of 1 lemon

shaved parmesan

excellent-quality olive oil, for drizzling

finely chopped flat-leaf (Italian) parsley
(optional)

## Method

Set the slow cooker to the sauté function. Add the butter and oil and, once hot and the butter is foaming, add the onion. Cook for 5 minutes until soft and fragrant, stirring often to prevent burning. Add the garlic and a good pinch of salt and cook for another 2 minutes. Add the mushrooms and herbs and turn the heat to low. (You may need to add the mushrooms in batches to prevent them overcrowding and stewing instead of browning.) Cook, stirring regularly, for another 5 minutes, then pour over the wine and stock. Close the lid and cook for 6 hours, removing the lid after 3 hours to allow some of the liquid to evaporate and the sauce to thicken.

Using a hand-held blender, give the ragu a quick blitz. You don't want to obliterate the mushrooms; just a very quick maceration will do the trick to break down any larger pieces. Serve as a bed for some pan-fried gnocchi or toss it through pappardelle. To finish, grate over the lemon zest, scatter with parmesan and drizzle over some superb-quality olive oil and the parsley, if using.

# Red wine beef cheeks with horseradish cream & saltbush

SERVES 4

These beef cheeks are set-and-forget glory; the greatest effort is probably overseeing the saltbush leaves in a frying pan just before serving. They look all kinds of fancy but really aren't. Saltbush can be a little hard to source, so if you are planning on cooking this dish for a special occasion, toddle off to your local grocer or deli and ask them to order it for you. Its crisp, salty tang makes it worth seeking out. If you can't find saltbush, simply omit and top with the baby watercress and a generous pinch of salt flakes.

This has to be one of my favourite dishes; the layers and contrasts between the rich meat, the cut-through of the horseradish and the salty tang of the saltbush make it rather spectacular.

If you were making it for a crowd, you could cook the beef cheeks then reduce the sauce on the day of serving and simply warm the beef again in the sauce right before serving.

## Ingredients

4 beef cheeks (approx. 1–1.2 kg/
 2 lb 3 oz–2 lb 10 oz)
1 tablespoon olive oil
1 onion, diced
2 garlic cloves, crushed
1 celery stalk, diced
1 carrot, diced
1 tablespoon tomato paste
 (concentrated purée)
2 bay leaves
250 ml (8½ fl oz/1 cup) beef stock
500 ml (17 fl oz/2 cups) red wine

## Horseradish cream

200 ml (7 fl oz) pouring (single/light) cream
2 tablespoons freshly grated horseradish

## To serve

2 tablespoons rapeseed oil
saltbush leaves
2 tablespoons baby watercress
freshly grated horseradish, to garnish
 (optional)

## Method

Wash and pat dry your beef cheeks. Set the slow cooker to the sauté function. Add the oil and, once hot, fry the onion for up to 5 minutes, or until soft and fragrant. Add the garlic, celery and carrot and cook for another 1–2 minutes, or until soft. Add the tomato paste and cook until the vegetable mix is thoroughly coated in the tomato. Add the beef cheeks (you may need to do this in batches to prevent overcrowding) and cook, turning regularly, to brown a little on all sides. Add the bay leaves, stock and wine, then close the lid and cook on low for 10–12 hours.

Gently remove the beef cheeks and set aside. Strain the residual braising liquid into a bowl to remove any chunks, then pour the liquid back into the slow cooker. Set to the sauté function and reduce the liquid by at least half – more if you want a thicker, more jus-like sauce. This could take 20–30 minutes.

While the sauce is reducing, make the horseradish cream. Whip the cream to soft–medium peaks, then gently stir through the horseradish. (You can do this the day before serving and place in an airtight container in the fridge.)

Place a frying pan over a high heat. Add the rapeseed oil and, once shimmering, add the saltbush leaves and fry for just 10–20 seconds on each side. Remove with a slotted spoon onto paper towel.

Return the beef cheeks to the reduced sauce briefly to warm through, then plate them up. Pour over the sauce and top with a dollop of horseradish cream garnished with saltbush and watercress, or serve the cream on the side.

# Twelve-hour pork & Sobrassada with tomato, white wine & pecorino

SERVES 6–8

For this recipe, you will need to roughly cut the pork into chunks. This is so you can sear it (sort of) in the slow cooker, and so the pieces fit a little more snugly in the bowl.

You can serve this with pasta or gnocchi – either works a treat.

## Ingredients

1½ tablespoons olive oil

1 onion, finely chopped

1 leek, washed, white part only, finely sliced

1 celery stalk, finely chopped

200 g (7 oz) mild Sobrassada (cured pork sausage), finely chopped

1 kg (2 lb 3 oz) boneless pork shoulder, cut into pieces

200 ml (7 fl oz) white wine

2 × 400 g (14 oz) tins chopped tomatoes

200 g (7 oz) black Ligurian olives, pitted

3 tablespoons marjoram leaves, finely chopped

## To serve

rigatoni, pappardelle or gnocchi

pecorino

marjoram or basil leaves

## Method

Set the slow cooker to the sauté function. Add the oil and, once hot, add the onion, leek and celery and cook for 15 minutes, stirring often, until very soft. Add the Sobrassada and cook for a further 5 minutes. Don't rush this step as you want the oils from the sausage to separate and the meat and aromatics to fully caramelise. Add the pork shoulder pieces and cook until they take on some colour around the edges. Add the wine, tomatoes and olives. Close the lid and reduce the heat to low. Cook for 12 hours. Open the lid and stir through the marjoram leaves.

Use a wooden spoon to gently break up the meat into the sauce. Alternatively, you can shred the meat in the bowl using a couple of forks.

Serve hot over your favourite pasta or gnocchi, scattered with plenty of pecorino and some extra marjoram or basil leaves. Season generously with salt and pepper.

# Tamari-braised pumpkin, sunflower cream & horseradish

SERVES 4

This is a slow cooker riff on a pumpkin recipe from Etta, a restaurant in Melbourne. The salty tamari is wondrous against the sweet pumpkin and gives this plenty of oomph as a standalone dish, but it does need all of its accompaniments to really make it sing. To that end, find some fresh horseradish – the bottled stuff will do at an absolute pinch, but it doesn't compare to the fresh root.

To make the sunflower cream, you need to soften the sunflower seeds in plenty of water. Soaking them for 6 hours ensures they are soft enough, but it's even better if you throw the seeds and water in a bowl the day before.

## Ingredients

120 g (4½ oz) brown sugar
170 ml (5½ fl oz/⅔ cup) tamari
60 ml (2 fl oz/¼ cup) olive oil
125 ml (4 fl oz/½ cup) vegetable stock
1 kg (2 lb 3 oz) jap or kent pumpkin
    (squash), skin on, cut into wedges,
    seeds discarded

### Sunflower cream

100 g (3½ oz) sunflower seeds, soaked
    in water for at least 6 hours
1 tablespoon vegetable stock
½ tablespoon lemon juice
60 ml (2 fl oz/¼ cup) each grapeseed oil
    and olive oil
60 g (2 oz/¼ cup) Persian feta

### To serve

dill fronds
salted pepitas (pumpkin seeds; optional)
freshly grated horseradish

## Method

Set the slow cooker to low and heat for at least 15 minutes. Add the sugar, tamari, oil and stock and cook, stirring regularly, until the sugar has dissolved. Gently add the pumpkin pieces and attempt to fit them as snugly as possible in a single layer. Cook for 1 hour, gently turning the pumpkin halfway through so it cooks evenly in the braising liquid.

Depending on the thickness of your pumpkin and the temperature of your slow cooker, I recommend checking this at the 45-minute mark to see how the pumpkin is progressing, and then checking at 15-minute intervals after that. It may take up to 2 hours to cook.

While the pumpkin is cooking, prepare the sunflower cream. Strain the sunflower seeds, add to a food processor or blender with the stock and lemon juice and a few tablespoons of water, then blitz to combine. If it seems really thick and is not moving easily, add a little more water, a tablespoon at a time (you don't want it to be runny). With the motor running, slowly pour in the oils until you achieve a smooth, mayonnaise-like consistency, adding a little more water if necessary, then season to taste with salt. Add the feta and blitz one last time.

Drizzle the sunflower cream onto a serving platter. Gently add the pumpkin pieces and top with the dill fronds, salted pumpkin seeds, if using, and season with salt and pepper. Grate over plenty of fresh horseradish and serve.

# Eton Mess with gin strawberries & Turkish delight

SERVES 6–8

You can make a pavlova-style meringue in the slow cooker. Sure, it might not have the mighty peaks, but the texture is pretty spectacular and works perfectly with this dessert. You want that decadent sponge-like mouthfeel, and that is what you achieve with the slow cooker, not the crisp exterior. Kids seem to love this one, so you can skip the gin if you have smaller mouths to feed.

## Meringue

5 egg whites

230 g (8 oz/1 cup) caster (superfine) sugar

1 teaspoon cornflour (cornstarch)

2 teaspoons vanilla bean paste

1½ teaspoons apple-cider vinegar

## Gin strawberries

60 ml (2 fl oz/¼ cup) gin

250 g (9 oz) strawberries, hulled, halved

1 teaspoon vanilla bean paste

2 teaspoons caster (superfine) sugar

300 ml (10 fl oz) thickened (whipping) cream

## Mix-ins

125 g (4½ oz) raspberries

250 g (9 oz) strawberries, hulled, halved

6 pieces rose Turkish delight, finely sliced

1–2 edible flowers, petals torn

## Method

Set your slow cooker to low. Line the bowl with a sheet of baking paper and prepare the meringue while it warms.

Beat the egg whites on high in the bowl of a freestanding electric mixer fitted with the whisk attachment until soft peaks form. Gradually add the caster sugar until fully incorporated. Don't rush this; add it very gradually, and check it has been incorporated by rubbing the mixture between two fingers. If it feels grainy, it needs to be beaten for longer. Sift over the cornflour, then whisk through the vanilla and vinegar. Your mixture should look glossy and pillowy. Pour into your prepared slow cooker bowl. Place a tea towel (dish towel) over the top and cover with the lid. Cook for 90 minutes, then take the lid off and cook for another 10 minutes. Turn off the slow cooker and allow the meringue to cool completely before removing. It will feel soft.

To make the gin strawberries, add the gin, strawberries, vanilla and sugar to a blender and give it a quick whiz. Store the purée in the fridge until ready to serve.

Whisk the cream in a bowl until soft peaks form, about 4–5 minutes, but do not overbeat. Add half the strawberry mixture, crumble over large chunks of meringue, then fold once or twice to just combine. Turn out onto a serving platter. Scatter over the raspberries, strawberries, Turkish delight and edible flower petals. Dollop over the remaining strawberry mixture. Serve immediately.

# Lamb shawarma

SERVES 4–6

I suggest doing this with a small leg of lamb as you get the best results by being able to lay the meat as flat as you can in the base of the slow cooker. This allows the braising liquid to come up the sides so that the glorious spicy crust can be maintained. Obviously, slow cooking a lamb leg is a far cry from roasting it on a rotisserie, but the spice-addled preparation is the same and the end result is freaking delicious. I love serving this as part of a spread with flatbreads, pomegranate, bundles of mint and tahini.

You will need a large, shallow-base slow cooker for this recipe

This works best if you can prepare it ahead. The day before you want to serve it, rub the spices into the scored meat and rest it in the fridge overnight.

## Ingredients

2 teaspoons black peppercorns

6 cloves

1 star anise

1 teaspoon cardamom seeds

½ teaspoon fenugreek seeds

1½ teaspoons fennel seeds

1 tablespoon cumin seeds

1 tablespoon coriander seeds

½ tablespoon ground cinnamon

1 teaspoon nutmeg

1 tablespoon sweet smoked paprika

½ tablespoon sumac

4 garlic cloves, crushed

zest of 1 lemon

1–1.2 kg (2 lb 3 oz–2 lb 10 oz) lamb leg, bone in

1 litre (34 fl oz/4 cups) chicken or vegetable stock, or enough to come three-quarters of the way up the side of the lamb

### To serve

tahini

pomegranate arils

finely sliced red onion (optional)

flatbreads

mint and coriander (cilantro) leaves

## Method

Add the peppercorns, cloves, star anise and all the seeds to a frying pan and briefly dry-roast over a medium–high heat until the spices pop and become fragrant. You can also do this in your slow cooker if you have it nice and hot. Grind them in a spice grinder or using a mortar and pestle. Add to a bowl with all the remaining ingredients, except the lamb and stock, and stir to combine.

Score the lamb leg in several spots. Rub the spices into the skin and top of the leg, then set aside to marinate for a minimum of 2 hours, but preferably overnight.

Set your slow cooker to low. Add the lamb, then gently pour the stock into the bowl, being careful not to pour it over the top of the lamb; you want to keep as much of the spice mixture on the meat as possible to form a crust. Cover and cook for 10 hours. Remove the lid for the last 30 minutes of cooking.

Let the lamb rest for 10 minutes before serving with tahini, pomegranate arils, red onion, if using, flatbreads and herbs.

# Poached salmon with chipotle, tamarind & maple

SERVES 6–8

You will need a large, shallow-base slow cooker for this recipe

It feels a bit criminal putting this here. It is so simple to make, yet completely luxurious to taste. The tang of the tamarind and the smokiness of the chipotle work wonders with the sweet salmon.

## Ingredients

80 ml (2½ fl oz/⅓ cup) rapeseed oil

3 shallots, grated

6 cm (2½ in) piece ginger, grated

3 cloves, toasted and roughly crushed

1 tablespoon cumin seeds, toasted and roughly crushed

2 teaspoons chipotle powder

1 teaspoon black peppercorns, toasted and roughly crushed

2 teaspoons coriander seeds, toasted and roughly crushed

2 tablespoons tamarind purée

3 tablespoons maple syrup

800 g–1 kg (1 lb 12 oz–2 lb 3 oz) side of fresh salmon, skin on, bones removed

375 ml (12½ fl oz/1½ cups) vegetable stock

## To serve

steamed coconut rice

stir-fried Asian greens

## Method

Set the slow cooker to the sauté function. Add 1 tablespoon of the oil and, once hot, add the shallot and ginger and cook until soft and fragrant, about 5 minutes. Gently scoop out the mixture into a bowl and combine with all of the spices, the tamarind and maple syrup and the remaining oil. Whisk, then taste and adjust the seasoning. Gently rub the mixture into the top side of the salmon.

Wipe your slow cooker bowl clean, then line it with baking paper. This makes it easier to remove the fish after cooking, otherwise it will collapse. Gently lay your piece of salmon in the cooker, tucking the tail in on itself to create an even fillet. Carefully pour the stock around the sides of the fish so it doesn't wash the marinade off the top. Close the lid and cook on low for 2 hours. Check it at the 1½-hour mark. You can actually remove it at any time from the 1-hour mark depending on how you like your salmon cooked. If you like it pink, go for a shorter cooking time. I suggest noting how long it takes the first time you make this recipe so you can get to know your slow cooker.

Serve with coconut rice and Asian greens.

# Elderflower & white chocolate pots de crème

SERVES 4–6

Elderflower and white chocolate truly belong together. The floral tang of the elderflower does a phenomenal job of balancing the sometimes cloying sweetness of white chocolate. Try to use an elderflower cordial that isn't overly sweet.

These would also be great made with yuzu or rosewater, and the best bit? They are good for entertaining a crowd as you can make them beforehand and store them in the fridge.

Before you fill your glasses or ramekins, check how they fit in your slow cooker. You can either cook them in batches or stack the ramekins on top of each other, although I prefer the consistency of results by having each ramekin submerged in the water bath directly rather than relying on the circulating steam to cook the ones on top.

## Ingredients

250 ml (8½ fl oz/1 cup) thickened (whipping) cream
125 ml (4 fl oz/½ cup) full-cream (whole) milk
2 teaspoons vanilla bean paste
4 large egg yolks
3 tablespoons caster (superfine) sugar
1 tablespoon elderflower cordial
200 g (7 oz) white chocolate, melted and cooled

## To serve

edible flowers (optional)

## Method

Bring the cream, milk and vanilla to a simmer in a saucepan over a medium heat, then remove and set aside to cool. Meanwhile, whisk the egg yolks and sugar in a bowl until pale and creamy. Stir through the elderflower cordial. Gradually beat in the cream mixture, whisking gently until incorporated, then whisk in the white chocolate.

Strain into a jug and stand until the foam settles, about 15 minutes, then spoon any remaining foam from the top. If there isn't any foam, don't panic; this will not happen every time and you haven't done anything wrong if it doesn't occur.

Divide the cream mixture between glasses or ramekins, then carefully place them inside your slow cooker. If you can't fit them in a single layer, you can balance the remaining ones on top. Using a jug, gently pour water into the base of the slow cooker until it comes about halfway up the sides of the ramekins. Place a few layers of paper towel across the top of the cooker before sealing the lid. Make sure the paper overhangs the sides so that it doesn't fall into your glasses/ramekins. Cook on low heat for 2½ hours.

The first time you make these I suggest checking on them at the 90-minute mark. The mixture should be resistant to the touch and only have the slightest wobble when you move the glass/ramekin. Allow to cool slightly in the slow cooker, then gently remove, cover tightly with plastic wrap and leave to cool completely in the fridge. Let them sit at room temperature for 20 minutes before serving. Top with edible flowers, if using.

# The Sweetest Thing

**YES, THE SLOW COOKER** can absolutely delve into dessert and baked-goods territory. While you will never get the rise of pillowy sponge cakes, you can use its heat and steam to glorious effect. Desserts cooked this way are dense, fudgy and infused with flavour, thanks to the low and slow cooking times.

# One-cup triple-choc brownies with raspberry salt

MAKES APPROXIMATELY 10

It's not the complexity of the recipe but the quality of the ingredients that creates an otherworldly brownie. Use superb-quality chocolate and cocoa powder here. Give it a bit more oomph with the raspberry salt and it will not disappoint. This version is dense and fudgy with that crackled top – just the way I like my brownies. Given the slow-cooked nature of the bake, you won't get a cake-like texture if that's what you are after, but you will get a wedge of brownie, solid and comforting when served in World Atlas–sized portions.

The shape of the bowl will have an impact on your cooking time, depending on the height and width, with wider, shallower bowls allowing for more heat, thereby reducing the cooking time.

## Ingredients

250 g (9 oz) butter, melted and cooled,
   plus extra for greasing
125 g (4 oz/1 cup) Dutch cocoa powder
150 g (5½ oz/1 cup) plain (all-purpose) flour
230 g (8 oz/1 cup) dark brown sugar
115 g (4 oz/1 cup) caster (superfine) sugar
1 tablespoon vanilla bean paste
175 g (6 oz/1 cup) chocolate chunks
   (mixture of milk, white and dark)
4 large eggs

## Raspberry salt

10 g (¼ oz/½ cup) freeze-dried raspberries
2 teaspoons raw (demerara) sugar
1 teaspoon salt flakes

## Method

Preheat the slow cooker on low while making the brownie mixture.

Add all the brownie ingredients to a bowl and, using a whisk, beat to combine. Grease and line the bowl of your slow cooker with baking paper. Pour the batter in and use the back of a wooden spoon to level out the top. Cook with the lid off for 2½ hours. The first time you make these, I recommend checking the brownie at the 2-hour mark. If you use a deep, round bowl, your batter will be thicker and your cooking time will likely be longer – anything up to 3 hours.

Allow to cool before slicing. When ready to serve, combine the raspberry salt ingredients in a small bowl, then sprinkle generously over the brownie.

Leftover brownies will keep in the fridge for up to 1 week.

# Slow-cooked quince, broken meringue & sweet mukhwas

SERVES 6–8

This recipe is based on a dessert I had in Paris at restaurant Chateaubriand. We had stood in line for hours waiting for a table. Dinner started at close to midnight and we were the last to make it in. We finished eating at three in the morning and, to this day, it is one of the most memorable meals I have had. One of the courses was a single beautiful, lightly charred plum, its cooked flesh covered in mukhwas (Indian candied fennel seeds). I've never forgotten it – it was so simple, yet so complex, and I have offered a slightly different spin on it here.

I really recommend serving this with some crème fraîche and even a squeeze of lemon juice. While there is lots of texture with the poached quince, the meringue and the crunch of the candied seeds, it is layers of sweet on sweet and the crème fraîche provides a very necessary cut-through. I also recommend smaller serves for this very reason.

You can just poach the quinces and omit the meringue and Indian fennel seeds and use the fruit as a base for all kinds of desserts, from pies and tarts and crumble, to adding gelatine and making your own quince paste.

## Ingredients

1 cinnamon stick

½ teaspoon green cardamom seeds,
  lightly crushed

2 star anise

½ tablespoon vanilla bean paste

375 g (13 oz) caster (superfine) sugar

3 large quinces, peeled (reserve the
  peels), cored and cut into large chunks
  (keep as close to quarters and halves as
  you can to ensure they hold their shape)

## To serve (optional)

20 g (¾ oz/1 cup) broken meringue shards

2 tablespoons sweet mukhwas (Indian
  candied fennel seeds)

185 ml (6 fl oz/¾ cup) crème fraîche

squeeze of lemon juice

## Method

Put the cinnamon, cardamom, star anise and vanilla in the bowl of your slow cooker. Add the sugar, 1 litre (34 fl oz/4 cups) water and the reserved quince peels and set to the sauté function. Cook until the sugar has dissolved. Add the quince and turn the heat to low, then cover and cook for 10–12 hours. The quince is ready when the poaching liquid looks a little syrupy and the quince is a glorious ruby pink colour.

Gently remove the quince pieces and place on serving plates. Strain the cooking liquid and reserve it for another use, such as making quince jelly. Scatter over the broken meringue and the mukhwas just as you serve. Dollop each serve with a generous dessertspoon or so of crème fraîche and a squeeze of lemon juice to finish.

# Espresso martini chocolate buckwheat torta caprese

### SERVES 8–10

D eath. By. Chocolate. It's a dream: the coffee, the dark chocolate and the pure, luxurious mouthfeel of it all ...

## Ingredients

170 g (6 oz) unsalted butter, cubed,
   plus extra for greasing
225 g (8 oz) dark chocolate,
   roughly broken
½ tablespoon vanilla bean paste
2 tablespoons vodka
2 tablespoons strong espresso
170 g (6 oz/¾ cup) caster (superfine) sugar
115 g (4 oz/½ cup) brown sugar
6 eggs
150 g (5½ oz/1 cup) buckwheat flour
2 tablespoons Dutch cocoa powder,
   plus extra for dusting

### To serve

crème fraîche or vanilla ice cream
   (optional)
dried orange slices (optional)

## Method

Grease and line a 22 cm (8¾ in) springform cake tin. Set your slow cooker to low.

Combine the butter and chocolate in a heatproof bowl and place over a saucepan of gently simmering water. Stir until melted and glossy, then remove from the heat and mix through the vanilla, vodka and espresso. Stir to combine, then set aside.

Add the sugars and eggs to the bowl of a freestanding electric mixer fitted with the whisk attachment and beat on high until pale, thick and creamy, about 4 minutes. Stir through the buckwheat flour and cocoa powder. Slowly pour in the chocolate mixture and stir to combine, being careful not to overwork the batter.

Gently pour into the prepared tin. Cut yourself a length of baking paper about 30 × 15 cm (12 × 6 in) to act as handles underneath the cake tin. This will help you lower the tin into the cooker and get it out again. Transfer the tin to the slow cooker then cover with a tea towel (dish towel). This will prevent any moisture from the cooker dripping onto the torta. If your slow cooker has a removable lid, set it slightly ajar. If it is attached and twists closed, merely set it down but do not lock it into position as you want some of the steam to escape. Cook for 2½ hours, then check its progress. Touch the top: if it feels lightly set and tacky to the touch but firmer around the edges, remove the tea towel and the lid and cook for an additional hour (if not, check on it again at 10-minute intervals). Turn the cooker off and, gently, using your handy handles, remove the tin from the bowl. This torta is quite delicate, so pop it in the fridge for 30 minutes to set before slicing.

When ready to serve, dust with cocoa powder and slice. Allow to come to room temperature before serving. Top with crème fraîche and dried orange slices, if using.

# Yuzu lemon pudding with lemon crumble

SERVES 4–6

A little bit of a spin on the old-school lemon pud'. Such a spectacular favourite and, here, the punch of yuzu adds a depth and complexity of flavour. I absolutely adore yuzu. It can be a little hard to source, so I have made this dish both with and without – just substitute with more lemon juice if yuzu is unavailable.

You will need a large, shallow-base slow cooker for this recipe

## Ingredients

150 g (5½ oz) butter, plus extra for
   greasing
260 g (9 oz) caster (superfine) sugar
zest of 1 lemon
3 eggs
150 g (5½ oz/1 cup) self-raising flour
100 ml (3½ fl oz) full-cream (whole) milk
60 ml (2 fl oz/¼ cup) each of yuzu juice
   and lemon juice
60 ml (2 fl oz/¼ cup) boiling water

## Crumble

110 g (4 oz/¾ cup) plain (all-purpose) flour
55 g (2 oz/¼ cup) caster (superfine) sugar
50 g (1¾ oz) butter
2 teaspoons lemon zest
¼ teaspoon baking powder

## To serve

dried edible flowers, for sprinkling
   (optional)
lemon slices (optional)

## Method

To make the crumble, combine all the ingredients in a bowl and use your hands to fully rub in the butter. Spread on a tray lined with baking paper and bake in the oven at 170°C (340°F) for 8–12 minutes, or until the mixture is looking golden. Set aside until ready to serve.

Generously grease the bowl of your slow cooker. Set the cooker to low to warm up while you prepare the pudding.

Cream the butter, 200 g (7 oz) of the sugar and the lemon zest in the bowl of a freestanding electric mixer fitted with the whisk attachment until creamy and pale. Add the eggs, one at a time, and beat until combined. Gently stir through the flour and milk until just combined. Pour the batter into the bowl of your slow cooker.

Combine the yuzu juice, lemon juice, boiling water and remaining sugar in a jug and gently pour over the batter. Cover the slow cooker with a tea towel (dish towel) and close the lid. This will prevent any moisture from the cooker dripping onto the pudding. Cook for approximately 1 hour 40 minutes. You want the top of the pudding to look cake-like and set, but not the bottom. The time this takes will vary between slow cookers, so if you are unsure, working quickly, remove the bowl from the slow cooker and give it a gentle wiggle. The top should hold firm, but you will get some movement due to the liquid underneath. Return to the cooker and continue to cook, checking every 10–15 minutes, until cooked to your liking (keep the cooker lid ajar for this last stage of cooking so you can check on it easily).

Given this is the style of pud' you can't remove from the cooker in once piece, I either take the entire bowl to the table or scoop onto individual plates. To serve, scatter over the baked crumble mixture and edible flowers, if using, and garnish with lemon, if using.

# Simple spiced rice pudding with completely over-the-top toppings

SERVES 6

This is my take on a dish from one of my all-time favourite restaurants, Gerard's Bistro in Brisbane. The pudding is straightforward but, laden with as many or as few adornments as you like, you can turn this into a complete showstopper.

## Ingredients

200 g (7 oz/1 cup) sushi rice

700 ml (23½ fl oz) full-cream (whole) milk (see Note)

2 teaspoons vanilla bean paste

85 g (3 oz) honey

½ teaspoon ground cinnamon

## To serve

mixed berries

dried lavender

fresh honeycomb

edible flowers

crystallised violets

## Method

Wash the rice until the water runs clear. Add to the bowl of your slow cooker with three-quarters of the milk and all the remaining ingredients, then give everything a good stir to combine. Cook for 1 hour with the slow cooker set to low. If you happen to walk past it while it's cooking, pop open the lid, give it a quick stir, then go about your business. (It doesn't matter if you don't do this; it just helps to prevent it catching as the absorption rate between sushi rice brands and the heat of your slow cooker can vary.)

Gradually stir through the remaining milk in small amounts and cook for another 15 minutes. It is important to add the milk slowly because the rate of absorption between rices can vary. This allows you to control the final consistency, which should be creamy and easily stirred with a spoon, but not runny.

You may need to cook this either side of the suggested cooking time above; the aim is for the milk to have been absorbed, the rice grains to be just tender and the whole mix to have a delightful, creamy consistency.

Spoon the warm pudding into serving bowls and top with all the toppings.

**Note** / Depending on your slow cooker and the rate of absorption, you may need up to another 500 ml (17 fl oz/2 cups) milk.

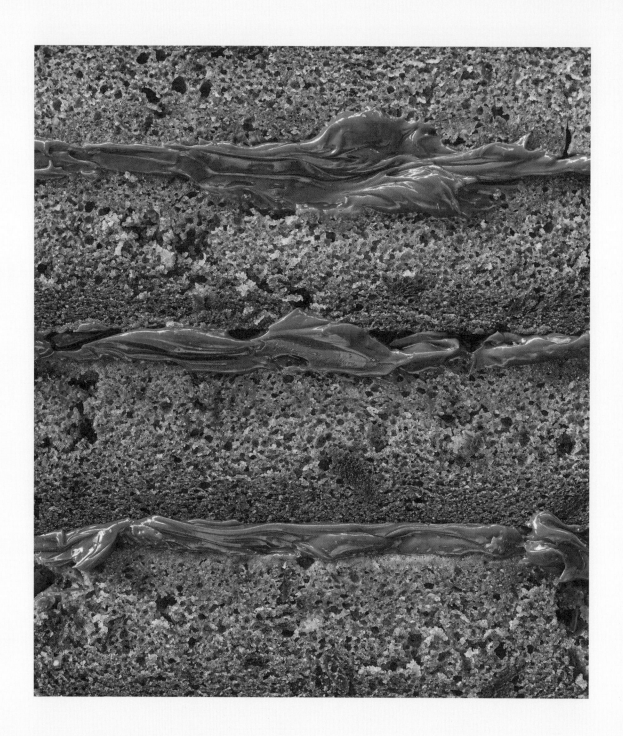

# Sticky date cake
# with dulce de leche

SERVES 8–10

Sticky date is such a perpetual favourite, so here is a make-and-pour version for the slow cooker, baked low and slow for 4 hours. The mouthfeel of the crumb is spectacular, given this is achieved without the heat and aeration of a regular oven.

## Ingredients

450 ml (15 fl oz) full-cream (whole) milk

2 teaspoons vanilla bean paste

180 g (6½ oz/1 cup) pitted dates, chopped

1 teaspoon bicarbonate of soda (baking soda)

150 g (5½ oz) unsalted butter, plus extra for greasing

220 g (8 oz) caster (superfine) sugar

3 eggs

225 g (8 oz/1½ cups) self-raising flour

## To serve

300 g (10½ oz) Dulce de leche (page 28, or use a quality shop-bought version)

salt flakes

## Method

Warm the milk and vanilla in a saucepan over a low–medium heat, watching closely to ensure it doesn't boil. Once warm, add the dates and cook over a low heat for about 3 minutes, or until the dates are beginning to soften. Remove from the heat. Add the bicarbonate of soda and set aside for 20 minutes while you prepare the rest of the cake.

Cream the butter and sugar in the bowl of a freestanding electric mixer fitted with the whisk attachment until light and creamy. Add the eggs, one at a time, until incorporated. Gently sift in the flour, then pour in the milk and date mixture. Whisk until combined, being careful not to overwork it.

Set the slow cooker to low and heat for about 5 minutes.

Grease and line the bowl of your slow cooker with baking paper (use a generous amount of paper so you can lift the cake out easily after cooking). Gently pour the batter into the bowl and place into the slow cooker. Cover with a tea towel (dish towel) before closing the lid (this will prevent any condensation dripping into your cake batter). Cook for 4 hours. Open the lid and allow to cool before gently removing the cake from the bowl. Cut into slices or thick wedges and smear with copious amounts of dulce de leche and a sprinkling of salt flakes.

If you are concerned about hot spots in your slow cooker, you can pour this batter into a lined 22 cm (8¾ in) springform cake tin (or one that fits inside your slow cooker) and put this in the bowl instead. In this case, cut yourself a length of baking paper about 30 × 15 cm (12 × 6 in) to act as handles underneath the cake tin. This will help you lower the tin into the cooker and get it out again. Follow the cooking times noted above. Using a cake tin may increase your cooking time slightly, as it is another layer of insulation between the heat source and the cake batter. Check for doneness at 15-minute intervals.

# Sparkling rosé
# poached peaches

SERVES 6

The sweetness of white peaches at their peak and the pure pink fizz of this dessert really encapsulate late summer eating at its best. The peaches are delightful on their own or with a dollop of crème fraîche.

You can, of course, cut the peaches in half and remove the stones, but I like throwing the whole lot in for a more low-maintenance approach. The stones are so easily removed once the peaches have slow-cooked, and it stops the fruit from losing its shape as it cooks.

## Ingredients

500 ml (17 fl oz/2 cups) sparkling rosé
115 g (4 oz/1 cup) caster (superfine) sugar
1 tablespoon rosewater
1 tablespoon vanilla bean paste
6 white peaches

## To serve

organic rose petals
3 tablespoons roughly crushed freeze-
   dried raspberries or strawberries

## Method

Combine the rosé, sugar, rosewater and vanilla in the bowl of your slow cooker. Set to the sauté function and cook for 10 minutes, stirring to dissolve the sugar. Turn the heat to low, add the peaches and close the lid. Cook for 2½ hours. Allow to cool completely in the syrup.

Gently remove the peaches and place in a large serving dish. Pour over the syrup, then scatter over the rose petals and the freeze-dried berries to serve.

# Spiced labne &
# baklava cheesecake

SERVES 8–12

Normally I am not a cheesecake lover – probably due to my lack of success in making a half-decent one. My preference has always been for the New York-style baked variety – I think they are far superior in texture and taste – but, when I make one, it always burns in spots, or splits due to uneven sugar distribution, no matter how long I mix the damn thing. Then I started testing in the slow cooker and it was a revelation. It is the perfect environment for cheesecake: steady heat and little to no evaporation with a result that is truly silky and a top that is free from cracks. Win-win.

## Crust

100 g (3½ oz) Marie biscuits, or similar
    tea biscuits
275 g (9½ oz) baklava, roughly chopped
120 ml (4 fl oz) melted butter (you
    may need more, depending on the
    consistency of your baklava; see
    method)

## Filling

350 g (12½ oz) cream cheese, at room
    temperature or a malleable consistency
115 g (4 oz/½ cup) caster (superfine) sugar
1 teaspoon ground cinnamon
½ teaspoon ground allspice
1 teaspoon ground cardamom
1½ teaspoons vanilla bean paste
2 large eggs
125 g (4½ oz/½ cup) labne
2 tablespoons milk powder

## To serve

pomegranate arils

## Method

For the crust, combine the biscuits and baklava in a food processor and blitz to a crumb. Tip into a bowl and add the melted butter, turning the mixture to coat and evenly distribute the butter. You may need to add a little more at this point; you want the mixture to hold its form. To check, roll some between your hands to form a clump or ball. If you press on it gently, you want it to hold. If it crumbles everywhere, add a little more butter, about 1 tablespoon at a time, until you reach the desired consistency.

Grease and line a 22 cm (8¾ in) springform cake tin. Gently press the crumb into the base and up the side. Place in the fridge while you prepare the filling.

Add all the filling ingredients to a food processor fitted with the blade attachment and pulse until smooth. Don't rush this part; you want everything to be fully incorporated. Pour over the crust and gently tap to remove any air bubbles.

Add the bowl to your slow cooker. Roll up some aluminium foil to create three large balls, about the size of a golf ball. Fill the slow cooker with water up to 5 cm (2 in) deep and place the foil balls in the cooker. These will stop the cheesecake sitting directly in the water and allow it to steam as it cooks. Make a 'sling' with a sheet of foil (about 30 × 15 cm/12 × 6 in) and place this under the tin. This will help you lower the tin into the cooker and out again. Gently lower the cheesecake into the cooker and place on the foil balls. Cover the top with a tea towel (dish towel) before closing the lid and securing it entirely. Cook for 2 hours on high. Let the cheesecake rest, covered, for 1 hour.

Place in the fridge to cool completely, preferably overnight, before serving.

Top with pomegranate arils to serve.

# Vanilla cardamom apricots with pistachio praline

SERVES 4–6

I'm obsessed with slow-cooked apricots; I love their sweet, soft nature and residual tang. Perhaps it's a hangover from my childhood – my grandmother made the ultimate apricot pie. I would do anything for just one more piece of it made by her loving hands.

The toffee crunch of the praline is a great contrast to the soft apricots, and the caramel toffee is a lovely friend to the warming spices in this dessert.

## Ingredients

1 tablespoon vanilla bean paste

6 green cardamom pods, bruised

12 apricots, halved

200 g (7 oz) caster (superfine) sugar

350 ml (12 fl oz) sticky white dessert wine

## Pistachio praline

200 g (7 oz) caster (superfine) sugar

1 teaspoon ground cardamom

80 g (2¾ oz) pistachio nuts, roughly chopped

## To serve

labne or mascarpone

dried rose petals, to garnish (optional)

## Method

Set the slow cooker to low and add all the ingredients for the apricots. Give it a gentle stir, cover with the lid and cook for 4 hours. Remove the lid and cook for another 30 minutes to allow the liquid to reduce slightly. Allow to cool completely in the bowl.

To make the pistachio praline, bring the sugar and 100 ml (3½ fl oz) water to the boil in a small saucepan over a medium–high heat. Brush down the sides of the pan with a wet pastry brush to remove any stray sugar. Reduce the heat to medium and cook until it becomes a lovely caramel colour, about 5 minutes. Stir through the cardamom and pistachio nuts (be careful as the mixture will spit). Pour onto a sheet of baking paper and set aside to cool, about 10–20 minutes. Break into shards and set aside.

When ready to serve, smear a plate with a generous amount of labne or mascarpone. Gently scoop out the apricots using a slotted spoon (being careful as they will be very soft) and place on top. Spoon over a few tablespoons of the poaching liquid, then top with pistachio praline and serve.

# Carrot & pistachio cake with spiced cream cheese frosting

SERVES 10–12

Slow cooking this style of cake with its heavier, wetter ingredients results in a dense yet entirely delightful cake.

I try to use ground black cardamom for this; the sweet, husky, smoky flavour seems to complement the sweeter profiles beautifully.

## Ingredients

360 g (12½ oz) coarsely grated carrot (about 2 carrots)
360 g (12½ oz) caster (superfine) sugar
75 g (2¾ oz) ground pistachio nuts
200 ml (7 fl oz) vegetable oil
4 large eggs, at room temperature
40 g (1½ oz/⅓ cup) sultanas (golden raisins), chopped
3 teaspoons baking powder
2 teaspoons ground cinnamon
2 teaspoons ground black cardamom (substitute with green cardamom if unavailable)
2 teaspoons ground cloves
175 g (6 oz) plain (all-purpose) flour
butter, for greasing

## Frosting

375 g (13 oz/1½ cups) cream cheese, at room temperature
1 teaspoon vanilla bean paste
30 g (1 oz/¼ cup) icing (confectioners') sugar
1 teaspoon ground black cardamom (substitute with green cardamom if unavailable)

## To garnish (optional)

honeycomb
pistachios, roughly chopped
dried orange and lemon slices
dried edible flowers
chunks of nut praline

## Method

To make the cake, add all the ingredients, except the flour, to a bowl and stir vigorously with a wooden spoon to combine. Add the flour and stir gently until fully incorporated.

Grease and line the bowl of your slow cooker, ensuring you have a generous overhang of baking paper so you can easily use the sides to pull the cake from the bowl once cooked. Pour the batter into the lined bowl and place in the slow cooker. Cover the top with a tea towel (dish towel) before closing the lid. Cook on low for 4 hours. After the cake has cooked, allow it to cool in the cooker for about 15 minutes before gently removing and leaving to cool completely. Once completely cooled, work carefully and cut the cake in half horizontally for icing. You can skip this step and just ice the top if you prefer.

For the icing, combine the ingredients in the bowl of a freestanding electric mixer fitted with the whisk attachment and beat until light and fluffy, about 2–3 minutes. Spread half the icing over the bottom half of cake, sandwich with the top, then spread the remaining icing over the top and sides. Top with honeycomb, pistachios, citrus slices, edible flowers and nut praline, if using.

This cake will keep relatively well, covered in an airtight container, for up to 3 days in the fridge.

If you are concerned about hot spots in your slow cooker, you can pour this batter into a lined 22 cm (8¾ in) springform cake tin (or one that fits inside your slow cooker) and put this in the bowl instead. In this case, cut yourself a length of baking paper about 30 × 15 cm (12 × 6 in) to act as handles underneath the cake tin. This will help you lower the tin into the cooker and get it out again. Follow the cooking times noted above. Using a cake tin may increase your cooking time slightly, as it is another layer of insulation between the heat source and the cake batter. Check for doneness at 15-minute intervals.

# Acknowledgements

Jane Willson: Jane, what can I say, we started off talking about salads and ended up with slow cooking. Thank you for allowing me such creative freedom with this project and entrusting me not only with the recipes but also the photography.

Anna Collett: Thank you for your constant and calm support and insightful feedback that always pushed this to be the best book it could be. Thank you for believing in me and for always (despite COVID) only ever being a phone call or email away.

Julia Murray: Thank you for your gorgeous design. The colour palate and layout are functional meets aesthetic perfection.

Andrea O'Connor: Thank you for steering this book on its course; and bringing it back when I drifted. It is consistent, accurate and a far better end product because of your keen eye. Thank you.

The Hardie Grant Team:
Marketing and publicity – thank you for shaping this and shouting about *Slow Victories* as the kind of book people need in their lives.
Design and production – the engine room. Thank you for working like the well-oiled and spectacular cogs that you are in this book-making machine, turning *Slow Victories* around in the way you have and getting it ready for the world.

Tom: Thank you. Love of my life. Life is busy, made busier by three small girls, and yet you always find the time to help make these projects come to fruition. This book would not be in existence if it wasn't for your support, taste testing, and ten million trips to the supermarket or farmers' markets for ingredients. Thanks for cleaning up messes that often extend far beyond the kitchen.

**Lulu, Claude, Eddie:** Slow cooker bowls are not weapons, nor helmets. And they are definitely not something you hide from me when I really, really need them. You live life to its limits, and I love you all for it. Everything I do is for you.

**Mum and Dad:** Thank you. For everything. Always. I love you. I try to live by your advice every single day – 'keep smiling and don't take shit from anyone'. Mum, you gave me a creative eye, and Dad, you passed on your cattle dog work ethic. I couldn't survive without either.

**Katie:** Hand model, wrangler of small children and kitchen manager. Thank you for your constant help keeping the wheels turning and mucking in whenever for whatever needed doing. I feel I have played a part in your future modelling career.

**My family and friends:** You know who you are. Thank you for lending me your ears, your bellies, your opinions and your laughter. Thank you for your honesty and for your unwavering belief in me.

**Readers:** Thank you for taking a leap of faith and buying this book. Whether you came across my work from other books, *Good Food* or just took a chance, books like this don't exist without those of you willing to buy them, cook from them and share them. Thank you from the bottom of my heart. Because of you I get to do what I love every single day, and that kind of privilege is not taken for granted.

# INDEX

Published in 2021 by Hardie Grant Books,
an imprint of Hardie Grant Publishing

Hardie Grant Books (Melbourne)
Building 1, 658 Church Street
Richmond, Victoria 3121

Hardie Grant Books (London)
5th & 6th Floors, 52–54 Southwark Street
London SE1 1UN

hardiegrantbooks.com

Hardie Grant acknowledges the Traditional Owners of the country on which we work, the Wurundjeri
people of the Kulin nation and the Gadigal people of the Eora nation, and recognises their continuing
connection to the land, waters and culture. We pay our respects to their Elders past, present and emerging.

A catalogue record for this
book is available from the
National Library of Australia

Slow Victories
ISBN 9781 74379 641 2

10 9 8 7 6 5 4 3 2 1

Publishing Director: Jane Willson
Project Editor: Anna Collett
Editor: Andrea O'Connor
Design Manager: Mietta Yans
Designer: Julia Murray
Photographer: Katrina Meynink, Kait Barker
Production Manager: Todd Rechner

Colour reproduction by Splitting Image Colour Studio
Printed in China by Leo Paper Products LTD.

The paper this book is printed on is from FSC®-certified forests and other sources. FSC® promotes
environmentally responsible, socially beneficial and economically viable management of the world's forests